HOW TO
SUCCESSFUL

YOUR LIFESTYLE DIET

KAREN SULLIVAN

Wellhouse Publishing Ltd

First published in Great Britain in 2002 by
Wellhouse Publishing Ltd
31 Middle Bourne Lane
Lower Bourne
Farnham
Surrey GU10 3NH

DISCLAIMER

The aim of this book is to provide general information only and should
not be treated as a substitute for the medical advice of your doctor or
any other health care professional. The publisher and author is not
responsible or liable for any diagnosis made by a reader based on the
contents of this book. Always consult your doctor if you are in any way
concerned about your health.

A catalogue record for this book is available from the British Library

ISBN 1 903784 04 2

Printed and bound in Great Britain by
Biddles Ltd., Surrey. www.biddles.co.uk

For Eleanor Daisy

Contents

Introduction

It often takes a health scare to make the majority of us look at our eating habits. And although many of us are aware that our diets are not all they should be, few of us make any real attempt to redress the balance. We have supermarkets full of good, fresh food, but most of us choose the easy options - ready-made meals, take-aways, fast food, junk food and snacks eaten on the run. The concept of healthy eating sounds rather laborious and tasteless, and who has time to prepare nourishing meals? What's more, everyone else appears to eat much the same kinds of food, without any apparent ill-effects, so why make changes when there seems to be no need?

The fact is that what you eat affects your health much more dramatically than you might imagine.

Food forms the building-blocks of every single system, cell and bone in our bodies, and it affects the way they work and renew themselves. While most of us can get away with an unhealthy diet for a while, there's no doubt that over time we will begin to pay the price. Here are just some of the reasons why:

- A joint report by the World Cancer Research Fund (WCRF) and the American Institute for Cancer Research (AICR) claims that 30-40 per cent of cancers may be caused by dietary factors.
- According to a study published in *The Lancet*, average sperm count in Britain fell from a high of 113 million per millilitre in 1940 to 66 million in 1990. If this trend continues we can expect infertility to become a mass epidemic by the middle of the 21st century. A huge number of studies show that nutrition is the main cause, with oestrogens in the water, our food and in the environment playing havoc with male fertility. Men with low vitamin C also have a markedly increased likelihood of genetic damage to their sperm. You may be past the point of wanting to start a family, but it's worth considering what the future holds for our children, and our children's children.
- The British Heart Foundation says that more than 300,000 people in the UK suffer a heart attack each year, and of those, 115,000 die. Heart disease is the number-one killer in the UK. Apart from smoking and lack of exercise, the main cause is diet. You might also be interested to learn that some 20 per cent of children show early signs of heart disease, again caused by diet. This is not a problem for the older generations alone.
- Osteoporosis (thinning of the bones) is a condition that normally affects the elderly, but studies show that low bone mass (bones that

are not strong enough) is becoming more and more common in younger members of society. This poses a great personal risk, but also affects the nation as a whole, as the cost of caring for disabled members of society skyrockets.

- Consider, too, what the food you are eating is doing to your body. Processed foods have little nutritional value and contain a huge number of chemicals, the effects of which are only just beginning to be made clear. Many additives have now been banned, but some - particularly tartrazine or E102 - have been linked to hyperactivity in children, allergies, asthma, migraines and even cancer. Scientists are investigating a possible link between aspartame (found in diet drinks) and changes in brain function. Caffeine is linked to peptic ulcers, insomnia, nervousness and birth defects.

- Don't forget the problems associated with overweight. Half the population of the UK is now considered to be clinically overweight (that number is even greater in the US), and the numbers are increasing dramatically. Overweight presents a serious risk to health, and common related conditions include high blood pressure, high cholesterol, an enlarged heart, diabetes and a much higher risk of heart disease.

And there's more. Many of us are unaware that the niggling health complaints from which we suffer, such as headaches, fatigue, PMS, sleep and skin problems, aches and pains, digestive disorders, memory problems, trouble conceiving, mood swings and even menopausal symptoms, are related to the food we eat. A poor diet means that everything in our bodies works less efficiently, and in a less balanced way. Unless we get the nutrients we need, in fresh, wholesome food, we will be heading down the slippery slope towards serious health problems.

In an age where self-help books are top of best-seller lists around the world, it's hard to work out why such a very basic component of health and wellbeing is being neglected. And believe me, it is. A new study claims that only 13 per cent of men and 21 per cent of women in the UK manage to eat the daily recommendation of five portions of fruit and vegetables, and sales of biscuits, crisps and other processed foods are on the increase. Many people do not bother with breakfast, and a recent survey shows that a huge number of people skip meals because of the frantic pace of their lives. The research, by the supermarket chain Sainsbury's, found that nearly 70 per cent of people regularly miss at least one meal a day. Six out of ten people surveyed said they were simply too busy to stop to eat.

One factor influencing our eating habits is obviously the overscheduled nature of our lifestyles. The prospect of preparing a healthy, nutritious meal after a busy day at the office, or while dealing with screaming kids, is a daunting one. In the end, we adopt a measure of self-preservation, cutting corners when we can. One of the areas that is most affected by this approach is our diet. And there are thousands of manufacturers and retailers lining up to meet the demand for instant meals that can be prepared with a minimum of fuss.

We've also adopted a rather extraordinary cost-cutting mentality when it comes to food. We demand cheaper food in larger quantities, a trend that has seriously lowered the overall quality of the food on offer.

But good food is a necessity, not a luxury, and by lowering the overall standard, we are further undermining our diets and our health.

There are a multitude of myths surrounding healthy eating, and most of them go back to just a couple of decades ago. Healthy eating brings to mind, for many of us, pulses, unpalatable 'whole' breads, boiled greens, muesli and an array of tasteless, unidentifiable vegetables. And fair enough. With a limited repertoire of cooking styles, an absence of ethnic influences and a restricted number of foods available, 'health food' was indeed something that the majority of consumers would want to avoid.

But all that's changed. We have fresh, interesting and exotic foods flown in from halfway around the world; we have exciting international chefs who have transformed healthy eating into an art form; we have a vast array of ingredients, from a wide variety of cultures, all available in local supermarkets. What's more, there are reputable manufacturers now producing appetising, healthy fare at reasonable prices. We can buy woks and omelette pans that make preparation easy, and we have microwaves, food processors, juicers and steamers to do much of the work for us. In fact, there is simply no excuse for opting out of the healthy eating revolution. We are talking delicious food that makes us look and feel good, and we can prepare it in much the same time that it takes to plonk a few ready-made meals into the oven.

And that's what this book is all about. Healthy eating is more than just a short-term trend for a few health-conscious individuals. It comprises a revolution in the way we view our lives and look after ourselves. It holds the key to a healthy, happy future, in which we experience the type of good health and wellbeing that all of us deserve. It's called *Lifestyle Diet* because healthy eating should be just that - a normal part of a healthy lifestyle.

It's easy to eat well, no matter what your budget or tastes. Once you understand the very basic concepts behind the elements that make food good or bad for us, you will find a whole new world opening up to you. Choosing, preparing and eating good food can be a sublime experience, and make a real difference to the way you feel.

There are no major life changes required in making the shift to healthy eating. With a little knowledge, the transition is easy. But like anything else in life, the more energy you give it, and the bigger a priority it becomes in your life, the more you will benefit. And in just a few short weeks, you'll begin to look and feel better than you may have felt in quite some time. Your future is in your hands, and it's up to you to grasp it.

Part One
A Question of Balance

One cannot think well, love well, sleep well, if one has not dined well.

Virginia Woolf

Chapter One

What Makes a Healthy Diet?

This is the nuts-and-bolts section of the book, but it's essential reading if you want to understand the basics of healthy eating. Once you understand which foods we need, and why, you'll have the tools you need to begin making changes.

Our bodies are complicated mechanisms, but their requirements are fairly straightforward. If anything, healthy eating is simple, relying on just a few fundamental principles.

The Essentials

There are seven principal nutrients that make up a healthy diet:
- Fats, carbohydrates and proteins (called macronutrients, which basically means big)
- Vitamins/minerals and other trace elements (called micronutrients because they are microscopic)
- Water
- Fibre.

A balance of all these nutrients ensures that our bodies heal, grow, renew and develop, and carry out all of the processes that are necessary for life.

Rather than go into an extensive description of each of these elements, it seems more practical to discuss what we really need to know here: why they are essential, how much we need, and what happens when we don't get enough.

Fat Facts

In Chapter Two we'll look at the confusing issue of fats in more detail, but for now it's important to understand what they do in the body, and why we need them.

Fat has had fairly bad press over the past few years, and you could be forgiven for thinking that an entirely fat-free diet is not only acceptable, but essential. Unfortunately, this sort of information is misleading and even dangerous.

Fat is one of the three essential macronutrients, and crucial to health.

Obviously, too much fat is unhealthy, but given the recent emphasis on low- and no-fat foods, you'd think we'd be seeing a rapid decline in heart disease and overweight. As you've probably gathered, the population has in fact become fatter. It's eating the *right* fats, rather than *no* fats, that will ultimately make a difference to health.

We need fat for energy. It is necessary for the smooth functioning of our bodies - in particular, our nervous systems. Fats contain the vitamins A, D and E, which are essential to many of our bodies' processes. For children, fat is even more important. When babies are breastfed, over 50 per cent of their calories come from fat. When babies are weaned on to table foods, they still need more fats than adults to ensure that they grow and develop properly.

Which Fat?

Unhealthy Fats

Saturated fats are the 'bad' fats, found in butter, lard, meat, hard cheeses and eggs, and they are the scourge of our modern diet. Too much saturated fat is linked with all sorts of diseases, including heart disease, asthma and eczema, stroke, obesity and cancer. Saturated fat clogs our arteries and prevents beneficial nutrients from being absorbed by our bodies.

Luckily, product labelling has made it much easier for us to assess the level of saturated fats in the foods we eat. That's not to say that we need to read the labels on *every* single thing we eat. Choose a few products from the supermarket shelves or your cupboard at home to get an idea of the types of products that are high in saturated fats. Fried foods, mayonnaise, pizza, burgers, many baked goods such as cakes and cookies, and cooked meats such as salami are all high in saturated fats. These types of foods need to be kept to a bare minimum.

Another type of bad fats are the 'trans-fats', which are produced when we hydrogenate oils - even healthy oils. Hydrogenation is the process used to turn liquid fats into hard fats. Margarine is a good example of this process. A perfectly good oil is heated to give it a firmer consistency; in other words to make it more solid. We've been convinced that margarine is better for us because it uses 'healthy fats'. However, the hydrogenation process changes the *nature* of the fat so that our bodies cannot make use of it. Worse, it blocks the body's ability to use healthy oils (see below). Trans-fats are used in all kinds of processed and baked food, including biscuits, pies, crisps and cakes. If you see the word 'hydrogenated' on the label, the product contains a trans-fat.

WHAT TO DO
● Choose foods that do not contain hydrogenated oils.

- Eat as few saturated fat products as possible. Trim the fat from your meat, and try not to eat red meats more than once or twice a week.

Healthy Fats
Unsaturated fats are broken down into two groups: polyunsaturates and monounsaturates. The polyunsaturates are found in vegetable oils, nuts, seeds and oily fish. The monos are found in olive oil, avocados, nuts and seeds, and rapeseed oil. The polys do not seem to cause damage in our bodies unless they are heated, at which point they become unstable and a little more problematic. The monos appear to do some actual good, by protecting against heart disease among other things.

Then we have the fatty acids, which are essential: these fall into three main categories, which sound like something intergalactic: Omega-3, Omega-6 and Omega-9 oils. We'll look at these in Chapter Two.

WHAT TO DO
- No more than a third of your total fat intake should be in the form of saturated fats.
- The remainder should be unsaturated, focusing on the foods that contain essential fatty acids (see page 40).
- Overall, fat should not form more than about 20% to 30% of our diets. At present, many diets are more than 60% or even 70% fat, much of it the wrong kind.

Putting It Into Practice
Does the prospect of giving up your Friday steak, or butter on your toast, fill you with horror? It's not necessary to give up the foods you enjoy. You simply need to have less of them. A steak once a week will do you no harm if the rest of your diet is healthy. Similarly, a scraping of butter on your toast in the morning, alongside some fruit and fresh juice, is a perfectly healthy meal. But if you are eating unhealthy fats throughout the day, it's time to look at some of the options.
- Olive oil is one of the healthy monounsaturated fats, and it can be used in a wide variety of ways. Drizzle it over warm bread (in much the same way that Mediterranean Europeans do) or over vegetables in place of butter. It can be 'flavoured' by steeping garlic cloves or any other herb or spice in it for several days.
- If cheese is your weakness, why not switch to goat's cheese instead, which is lower in fat and easier on the heart? Or try something different, like hummus, bananas, roasted vegetables, poached salmon or lean ham in your sandwiches instead. Aim for variety, using many different types of foods, and you'll be much less likely to overdo it.

- Swap your frying pan for a wok, and stir-fry foods with a little bit of olive oil. Alternatively, try steaming, roasting or grilling, all of which cut down on the fat content of your food.
- Try some of the meat substitutes such as tofu or Quorn (go for the non-GM brands if you can). In sauces and stews they taste much like the real thing, and can make a difference to a healthy diet.
- Add fish to your menu. It's high in the essential fatty acids (EFAs) and low in saturated fats. If you can swap a meat meal for fish or another lean white meat, such as chicken, you'll be taking a step in the right direction.

The Power of Protein

Like fat, protein is essential for our diets, but we tend to get too much of it. One of the latest fads is a protein-only diet, which claims to encourage massive weight loss. It probably *will* make you lose weight, but at a cost. Protein diets are dangerous, and can lead to serious malnutrition. You need to aim to reduce protein in your diet, and to focus on the healthy forms, rather than overdo it or go too far in the other direction and cut it out entirely.

What Are Proteins?
- About 17% of the body is made of protein, including the muscles, bones, skin, nails and hair.

Proteins are made up of different combinations of 22 separate amino acids which our bodies need to function and, of course, to carry on living!
- A lack of protein in the diet causes a decrease in energy.
- Excess protein puts a strain on the liver and the kidneys and leads to an increased risk of certain cancers and heart disease.
- Almost all unrefined foods are loaded with proteins - some of the richest sources may surprise you! Oranges and rice are, for example, 8% protein, potatoes are 10%, and beans are 26%. Wheat and oatmeal come in at an astonishing 16%.

Healthy Proteins
Traditionally it has been believed that protein came from meat and other animal products. In fact, experts now say that the healthiest proteins (because they are lower in fat and normally contain many other nutrients) are those found in vegetable products.
- Animal proteins: Beef, pork, lamb, bacon, ham, sausages, chicken, turkey, game, fish and seafood, milk, butter, cheese and eggs

- Vegetable proteins: Quorn and other meat substitutes, tofu, pasta, string beans, broccoli, seedless raisins, sweetcorn, black beans, pulses, brown rice, sweet cherries, oranges and bananas, among others

WHAT TO DO
- Choose vegetable proteins over animal proteins wherever possible.
- When you do have animal proteins, go for those that are lower in saturated fats. From best to worst, these are:

Wild birds	*Game*	*Chicken*
Eggs	*Butter*	*Lamb*
Beef	*Dairy products*	*Pork*

Putting It Into Practice
- Meats with all visible fat cut off are much leaner, and much healthier sources of proteins than, say, marbled meat.
- The best proteins are those found in vegetable sources.
- Most healthy adults need between three and five *small* servings of protein a day - no more.
- Protein is essential, but we normally get far more than we need.

Carbohydrate Power

Carbohydrates are as wildly different as fats. The good carbohydrates are crucial for our health. The bad ones form a great deal of our 'junk food' intake, and they tend to act as 'anti-nutrients', which means that they undo all the good effects of the healthy foods we are eating.

Carbohydrates are energy food, and they are the body's main source of fuel. There are two main kinds: refined and complex (unrefined).

Good Carbohydrates
Complex carbohydrates include:

Fruit and vegetables	*Wholemeal unrefined flour*
(and their juices)	*Brown rice*
Wholemeal pasta	*Wholegrain breakfast cereals*
Wholemeal bread	*Pulses*
Porridge oats	*Barley*

The message is to eat *unrefined*. Complex carbohydrates supply a sustained source of energy, which means that they take longer to digest and assimilate. Unrefined foods contain vitamins and minerals, and proteins as well, making them excellent forms of balanced nutrition. If it's white, it's not likely to do you any good at all.

15

And the Bad ...

Unrefined carbohydrates supply energy, but they are quickly assimilated, causing a sudden energy boost and a subsequent fall. If you've ever suffered from a mid-afternoon dip of energy, you'll know what I mean. They fill you up, but they don't last very long. You'll need another meal or snack to keep things going. This all has to do with blood sugar. Refined carbohydrates send your blood sugar soaring, but it peaks and falls sharply very soon after your meal. Blood sugar problems lead to cravings, irritability, lethargy and feeling hungry a short time after a meal. On the other hand, unrefined, or complex, carbohydrates release energy more slowly, which has a much more balancing effect on blood sugar levels.

Quite apart from the blood sugar issue, refined carbohydrates have had the majority of their nutrients stripped from them in the refining process. Almost all chromium, for example, is lost when flour is refined. Chromium is the mineral that governs our glucose (sugar) tolerance levels. Other big losses are calcium, B vitamins, iron, zinc and potassium.

Unrefined carbohydrates include:

White sugar (and everything that contains it, including sweets, fizzy drinks, squashes, jams and jellies, cakes, biscuits, chocolate, breakfast bars, breakfast cereals, pies, tarts and most baked goods - the majority of some children's diets)

White flour (and everything that contains it, including bread, pasta, breakfast cereals, crackers, biscuits, cakes and pies)

White rice

WHAT TO DO
- We need between four and nine servings of healthy carbohydrates every day.
- About 60% of our diet should be made up of these healthy carbohydrates.
- Choose a variety of unrefined carbohydrates. White, refined carbohydrates have virtually nothing to offer.

Charting Your Intake
Sometimes it helps to visualise just how much of your intake should be taken in the form of the three main nutrients. This is how it should work out:

60% carbohydrates   *20-30% fats*   *10-20% protein*

Now work out how your diet matches this. Chances are you'll be getting too much fat, too much protein, and not enough carbohydrates. This imbalance can lead to health problems and, in particular, overweight. If you get the balance right, you'll be well on the way to achieving good health and wellbeing.

Fibre

Fibre is a relative newcomer to the key nutrient list, and its importance in our diets is often underestimated. Confusingly, fibre does not actually provide any nutrients. Instead, it has a host of roles in our bodies that encourage them to function properly.

- Anything that contains fibre requires considerable chewing. This stimulates the flow of saliva, which protects our teeth and encourages healthy digestion.
- Fibre literally acts as a broom in our bodies, clearing away debris from the digestive tract and keeping it healthy.
- It also adds bulk to our diet, which helps nutrients to be absorbed more efficiently.
- Pectin, which is a soluble fibre found in apples and carrots, is particularly important. It absorbs heavy metals such as lead and prevents them from being absorbed. Pectin also helps our bodies to eliminate waste products, and prevents the reabsorption of toxins in the bowel.
- The two main types of fibre are *soluble* (found in fruits, vegetables and grains such as oats and barley) and *insoluble* (found in wheat and wheat bran). The best fibre is soluble fibre, which is easier on the digestive tract and less likely to cause irritation.
- Fibre is an excellent way to prevent constipation, and most experts believe that it can substantially reduce the risk of bowel cancer, although this theory was recently disputed. Whatever the outcome of the studies that have been set up to challenge this assertion, there is no doubt that fibre has been positively linked with the prevention of such health conditions as heart disease, diabetes, haemorrhoids, IBS (irritable bowel syndrome) and appendicitis.

WHAT TO DO
If you can get the minimum of five to seven fruits and vegetables a day, you'll be well on your way to meeting your fibre needs.

Combine that with a shift away from refined foods (see page 16), in favour of those that are 'whole' or unrefined (wholemeal bread and pasta, for example), and you should be getting all you need.

- Peels, such as those found on apples, potatoes, pears and plums, are the most fibre-rich part of these foods. Leave them on whenever possible to boost your fibre intake. Experts recommend that we peel non-organic fruits and vegetables because of the number of toxins concentrated in the skin. Choose organic wherever you can, and wash carefully, but even with non-organic foods scrubbing is always better than throwing the peels away.

- Whole fruits are richer in fibre than juices, so although a glass of fruit juice will count as a fruit serving, you should consider at least two or three whole fruits a day to ensure that your fibre needs are met.
- Raw fruits and vegetables have more fibre than cooked, so try to eat some foods raw. Obvious choices are broccoli, carrots, celery, peppers, cucumbers and even sweetcorn, tinned in water. Choose these foods as snacks, with a dip if you like.
- Sprinkle beans or lentils into soups and on to salads. Add them to casseroles, soups, stews and even pasta sauces.
- Brown-rice crackers are a great source of fibre, and they are an ideal snack, either on their own or spread with a little whole-fruit jam, hummus, goat's cheese or other favourite topping.
- Healthy breakfast cereals are also a great source of fibre. Try to encourage oatmeal for breakfast to kick-start the day. Breakfast cereals don't always have to be for breakfast, either. Try porridge for supper or even a late-night snack.
- Add raisins, sesame seeds, sunflower seeds and dried fruits such as apricots, bananas and cranberries to your cereal, to bump up fibre content and increase its nutritional value.

Fibre-rich foods include apples, carrots, pears, bananas, dried fruits, sweet potatoes, beets, broccoli, cabbage, green beans, oatmeal, peppers, peas, potatoes, sesame seeds, squash, strawberries and wholegrains.

Water

About 65% of our bodies are made up of water, so it's not surprising that water is the most essential element of our diets. Without food we can last for several weeks. Without water, we'd be dead within a few days.

What Does it Do?
- Water is essential to the digestive process. If we don't drink enough between meals, the saliva flow slows down and digestion is less efficient.
- Almost 2 litres of water is excreted from our bodies every day through our skin, urine, lungs and gut, and many toxins are removed from our bodies this way. If we are losing this much water, we need to replace it. The more water we drink, the greater the number of toxins eliminated.
- Without water our cells cannot build new tissue efficiently, toxic products build up in our bloodstream, and blood volume decreases so

that we have less oxygen and fewer nutrients transported to our cells, all of which can leave us weak, tired and at risk of illness.

How Much Do We Need?
Aim to have a good litre or two a day. That might sound like a lot, but if you get into the habit of carrying a bottle with you and sipping throughout the day, it's easy to drink enough. Remember that coffee, tea and colas contain caffeine, which acts as a diuretic. If you are a big tea drinker, for example, you'll need to increase your water intake correspondingly.

See Chapter Five for more information on healthy drinking.

Vitamins, Minerals and Other Important Nutrients

So many claims have been made by neutraceutical companies over the past decade that most of us have become wary of and even bored by these nutrients. We've been rather beguiled into thinking that popping pills is the perfect antidote to an unhealthy diet, and happily consume billions of pounds' worth every year. In Chapter Six we'll look at the supplement story and work out exactly what is required and when. For now, however, we need to understand why these nutrients are so important to health.

The simple answer is that they are absolutely crucial to every single body process. An average Western diet, based on commercially produced and processed foods and low on the fresh, natural stuff, falls shockingly short of even the most basic recommended levels of vitamins and minerals. Many experts believe that this shortfall is a major contributory factor to many modern-day diseases.

It's not surprising, therefore, that a lucrative and important industry has built up around vitamins, minerals and other supplements. Below we'll look at the different vitamins and minerals that we need in our diet. I've noted for each the daily recommended dosage (called, confusingly, both RDA and RNI), but it can be hard to work out the levels found in different foods. Use this as a guide if you are thinking of supplementing (see Chapter Six), but try to eat at least one of the foods listed for each nutrient (and many foods contain lots of different ones) to ensure that you are getting enough.

Vitamin A
EU RDA 800 mcg (2700 IU)
US RDA 5000 IU
A fat-soluble vitamin which comes in two forms: retinol, found in animal products, and beta-carotene, which our body converts into vitamin A when we need more. Beta-carotene is found in bright-coloured fruits and vegetables.

Properties
- Anti-carcinogenic
- Prevents and treats skin disorders and ageing of skin
- Improves vision and prevents night blindness
- Improves our bodies' ability to heal
- Promotes growth of strong bones, hair, teeth, skin and gums
- May help in the treatment of hyperthyroidism

NOTES
- The RDA is believed to be inadequate, and people with special needs (following illness, suffering from infections, with diabetes, for example) should have a higher level.

Vitamin A as retinol is toxic and should not be taken at all by pregnant women. Beta-carotene is not toxic and is considered to be safe for adults and children alike.

Best Sources

Vitamin A   *Cod liver oil, liver, kidney, eggs and dairy produce*

Beta-carotene *Carrots, tomatoes, watercress, broccoli, spinach, cantaloupe, apricots*

B1 (Thiamine)
EU RDA 1.4 mg
US RDA 1.2-1.5 mg
Involved in all key metabolic processes in the nervous system, the heart, the blood cells and the muscles.

Properties
- Protects against imbalances caused by alcohol consumption
- May be useful in the treatment of neurological disease (particularly those caused by B1 deficiency)
- May help to treat anaemia
- May help to control diabetes linked to deficiency
- Helps to convert sugar to energy in the muscles and bones

Best Sources
Pork, milk, eggs, whole grains, organ meats, brown rice, barley

B2 (Riboflavin)
EU RDA 1.6 mg
US RDA 1.7 mg
A water-soluble member of the B-complex family of vitamins. It is crucial to the production of body energy and has antioxidant qualities. Riboflavin is not stored in any significant amount in the body, and deficiency is common.

Properties
- Works with enzymes to metabolise fats, protein and carbohydrates

- Aids vision
- Promotes healthy skin, hair and nails
- Promotes healthy growth and reproductive function
- Boosts athletic performance
- Protects against anaemia

NOTES
- Pregnancy, breastfeeding, taking the pill and heavy drinking all call for an increased intake.

Riboflavin is non-toxic in most doses, but it is not recommended that you take in excess of 400 mg per day, unless supervised by a registered practitioner.

Best Sources
Milk, eggs, fortified breads and cereals, green leafy vegetables and fish

B3 (Niacin)
EU RDA 15-18 mg
US RDA 13-18 mg adults, 5-6 mg infants, 9-13 mg children under 10
Niacin takes the form of nicotinic acid and nicotinamide, and is a fairly recent addition to the family of B-complex vitamins, named as a vitamin only in 1937.

Properties
- Helps prevent and treat schizophrenia
- Aids in cell respiration
- Produces energy from sugar, fat and protein
- Maintains healthy skin, nerves, tongue and digestion
- May lower cholesterol and protect against heart disease
- Reduces blood pressure
- May help to prevent diabetes

NOTES
- Large doses may be used therapeutically, but should be taken under the supervision of a doctor or practitioner.
- In high doses, niacin may cause depression, liver malfunction, flushing and headaches.

Best Sources
Meat, fish, wholegrain cereals, eggs, milk, cheese

B5 (Pantothenic Acid)
EU RDA 6 mg
US RDA 10 mg
A water-soluble member of the B-complex family of vitamins which helps maintain normal growth and the health of the nervous system.

Properties
- Necessary for brain functioning
- Encourages healing of wounds
- Helps in the production of energy
- Helps to reduce stress levels
- Controls metabolism of fat
- Encourages the immune system
- Prevents fatigue
- Lowers cholesterol levels and protects against heart disease
- Prevents and treats arthritis

Dosage
- No known toxicity; doses of over 300 mg per day should be supervised by a practitioner. Some people report stomach upsets at doses higher than 10 g.

Best Sources
Yeast, organ meats, eggs, brown rice, wholegrain cereals, molasses

B6 (Pyridoxine)
EU RDA 1.6-2 mg
US RDA 2 mg
Necessary for vitamin B12 to be absorbed. Required for the functioning of more than 60 enzymes in the body and for protein synthesis. Of all the B-vitamins, B6 is the most important for a healthy immune system.

Properties
- Boosts immunity
- Helps to control diabetes
- Assimilates proteins and fats
- Helps prevent skin and nervous disorders
- Treats symptoms of PMS and menopause
- Acts as a natural diuretic
- Protects against some cancers

NOTES
- Should always be taken as part of a B-complex supplement, and in equal amounts with B1 and B2.
- Vitamin B6 is toxic in high doses, causing serious nerve damage when taken at quantities of more than 2 g per day. Some people report side-effects with doses as low as 100 mg.

Best Sources
Meat, fish, milk, eggs, wholegrain cereals, vegetables

Vitamin B9 (Folic Acid)
EU RDA 200-360 mcg
US RDA 400 mcg
Also known as vitamin Bc. Low levels of folic acid may lead to anaemia. Folic acid is essential for the division of body cells, and needed for the utilisation of sugar and amino acids. Taken from just before conception, and particularly in the first trimester of pregnancy, folic acid can prevent spina bifida.
Properties
- Improves lactation
- May protect against cancer
- Improves skin
- Natural analgesic
- Increases appetite in debilitated patients
- Needed for metabolism of RNA and DNA
- Helps form blood
- Builds up resistance to infection in new-borns and infants
- Prevents spina bifida
NOTES
- There are many people at risk of deficiency, including heavy drinkers, pregnant women, elderly people and those on low-fat diets. Supplementation at 400-800 mcg is recommended for those at risk.
- Folic acid is toxic in large doses and can cause severe neurological problems.
Best Sources
Green leafy vegetables, wheatgerm, nuts, eggs, bananas, oranges and organ meats

B12 (Cobalamin)
EU RDA 2 mcg
US RDA 3 mcg
Cobalamin is essential for a healthy metabolism of nerve tissue, and deficiencies can cause brain damage and neurological disorders. Vitamin B12 was once considered to be a 'wonder drug' and was given by injection to rejuvenate.
Properties
- Improves memory and concentration
- Increases energy
- Necessary for maintenance of the nervous system
- Promotes healthy growth in children
- Protects against allergens and toxic elements
- Required to utilise fats, carbohydrates and proteins

Dosage
- Although Vitamin B12 is not considered to be toxic, it is not recommended that you take more than 200 mg daily, unless you are under the supervision of a registered practitioner.

Best Sources
Liver, beef, pork, eggs, cheese, fish and milk

Vitamin C
EU RDA 60 mg
US RDA 60 mg
Water-soluble, which means that it is not stored by the body and we need to ensure that we get adequate amounts in our daily diets. Vitamin C is also known as ascorbic acid, and it is one of the most versatile of the vitamins we need to sustain life. It is one of the antioxidant vitamins and is believed to boost immunity and to help fight cancer and infection.

Properties
- Acts as a natural antihistamine
- Antioxidant
- Boosts immunity and reduces the duration of colds and other viruses
- Helps to fight cancer
- Helps maintain good vision
- Maintains healthy bones, teeth and sex organs
- May help to overcome male infertility
- Reduces cholesterol and helps prevent heart disease
- Speeds up healing of wounds

NOTES
- Daily dosages of up to 1,500 mg per day appear to be safe, but take in three doses, preferably with meals and in a time-release formula.
- Vitamin C may cause kidney stones and gout in some individuals. Some people suffer from diarrhoea and cramps at high dosages, although the vitamin is considered to be non-toxic at even very high levels.

Best Sources
Rosehips, blackcurrants, broccoli, citrus fruits, and all fresh fruits and vegetables

Vitamin D
EU RDA 5 mcg
US RDA 10 mcg
Vitamin D is known as the 'sunshine' vitamin. Vitamin D can be produced in the skin from the energy of the sun, and it is not found in rich supply in any food. Deficiency is caused by inadequate exposure to sunlight, and

low consumption of vitamin D-containing foods.

Properties
- Helps protect against osteoporosis
- Boosts the immune system
- Helps protect against cancer
- Necessary for strong teeth and bones

NOTES
- Vitamin D is the most toxic of all the vitamins, causing nausea, vomiting, headache and depression, among others. Do not take in excess of 10 mcg daily.

Best Sources
Animal produce, such as milk and eggs, oily fish, butter and cheese. Cod liver oil is also a good source.

Vitamin E
EU RDA 10 mg
US RDA 30 IU
Fat soluble and one of the key antioxidant vitamins (see page 75). Apart from its crucial antioxidant value, vitamin E is important for the production of energy and the maintenance of health at every level.

Properties
- Accelerates healing - particularly of burns
- Alleviates fatigue
- Antioxidant, which helps to slow the process of ageing
- Boosts immunity
- Protects against cardiovascular disease
- Protects against neurological disorders
- Reduces symptoms of PMS
- Treats skin problems and baldness

NOTES
Vitamin E is non-toxic, even in high doses, but it is not suggested that you take in excess of 350 mg a day unless you are supervised by a registered practitioner.

Best Sources
Wheatgerm (fresh), soya beans, vegetable oils, broccoli, leafy green vegetables, whole grains, peanuts and eggs

Vitamin K
EU RDA none
US RDA none
The K vitamins are fat-soluble, and are necessary for normal blood clotting. They are often used to treat the toxic effects of anti-coagulant drops

such as Warfarin, and in people who have a poor ability to absorb fats.
Properties
● Controls blood clotting.
Best Sources
Vegetables such as cauliflower, spinach and peas, and wholegrain cereals

Boron
EU RDA none
US RDA none
Boron is a trace mineral found in most plants, and it is essential for human health. Recent research has reported that boron added to the diets of post-menopausal women prevented calcium loss and bone demineralisation - a revolutionary discovery for sufferers of osteoporosis.
Properties
● External treatment of bacterial and fungal infections.
● Lowers the incidence of arthritis
● Prevents osteoporosis
● Used to build muscles
NOTES
● Boron can be toxic, with symptoms including a red rash, vomiting, diarrhoea, reduced circulation, shock and then coma. A fatal dose is 15-20g, 3-6g in children. Symptoms appear at about 100 mg.
Best Sources
Root vegetables (such as potatoes, parsnips and carrots) grown in soil that is rich in boron.

Calcium
EU RDA 800 mg
US RDA 800-1,200 mg
Calcium is an important mineral, and recent research shows that many of us get only about one-third of what we need for good health. Calcium is essential for human life - it makes up bones and teeth, and is crucial for messages to be conducted along nerves, among other things.
Properties
● Alleviates cramps in the legs
● Encourages regular beating of the heart
● Helps to prevent heart disease
● Necessary for nerve impulse-transmission and muscular function
● Helps prevent cancer
● Soothes insomnia
● Treats and prevents osteoporosis
● Useful in the treatment of high blood pressure

- Useful in treating arthritis

NOTES
- More calcium is needed by women after the menopause, and while pregnant and breastfeeding.
- Doses over 2,000 mg per day may cause hypercalcaemia (calcium deposits in the kidneys), but since excess calcium is excreted this is unlikely to occur unless you are taking excess quantities of Vitamin D alongside.

Chromium
EU RDA none
US RDA none
Chromium is an important regulator of blood sugar.
Properties
- Aids in the control and production of insulin
- Aids in the metabolism of carbohydrates and fats
- Controls blood cholesterol levels
- Stimulates the synthesis of proteins
- Suppresses hunger pains

NOTES
- There is no RDA, but it is suggested that 25 mcg per day is adequate.

There is no evidence that chromium is toxic, even in high doses, since any excess is excreted.
Best Sources
Wholegrain cereals, meat and cheese, brewer's yeast, molasses and egg yolk

Cobalt
EU RDA none
US RDA none
An essential trace mineral which is a constituent of vitamin B12. The amount of cobalt you have in your body is dependent on the amount of cobalt in the soil, and therefore in the food we eat. Most of us are not deficient in cobalt, although deficiency is much more common in vegetarians.
Properties
Cobalt can, with vitamin B12:
- Help to prevent pernicious anaemia
- Help in the production of red blood cells
- Aid in the synthesis of DNA and choline
- Encourage a healthy nervous system
- Maintain myelin, the fatty sheath that protects the nerves

NOTES

When used therapeutically, side-effects occurred at doses above 30 mg; these included goitre, hypothyroidism and heart failure.

Best Sources

Fresh leafy green vegetables, meat, liver, milk, oysters and clams

Copper

EU RDA 1.2 mg

US RDA 1.5-3 mg

An essential trace mineral necessary for the act of respiration - iron and copper are required for oxygen to be synthesised in the red blood cells. Also important for the production of collagen, which is responsible for the health of our bones, cartilage and skin.

Properties

- Protects against cardiovascular disease
- Useful in the treatment of arthritis
- Boosts the immune system
- Acts as an antioxidant

NOTES

- Copper appears in good multi-vitamin and mineral supplements, and could be taken alone up to 3 mg a day.
- Excess intake can cause vomiting, diarrhoea, muscular pain and dementia.

Best Sources

Animal livers, shellfish, nuts, fruit, oysters, kidneys and legumes

Fluorine

EU RDA none

US RDA 1 mg fluoride 3.6 mg sodium fluoride

A trace mineral found naturally in soil, water, plants and animal tissues. Its electrically charged form is *fluoride*, which is how it is usually referred to. Fluoride supplements should always be taken with calcium.

Properties

- Protects against dental decay
- Protects against and treats osteoporosis
- May help to prevent heart disease

NOTES

- Major source is the drinking water, and typical daily intake is 1-2 mg. Tablets and drops are available from pharmacies, but should be limited to 1 mg daily in adults, and .25-5 mg for children. Do not supplement fluoride without the advice of your dentist.

- An excess of fluoride causes fluorosis, characterised by irregular patches on the enamel of the teeth, and depresses the appetite.

Best Sources
Seafood, animal meat, fluoridated drinking water and tea

Iodine
EU RDA 150 mcg
US RDA 80-150 mcg
A mineral first discovered in 1812 in kelp. Iodine was extracted and given its name because of its violet colour. Iodine occurs naturally and is a crucial part of the thyroid hormones which monitor our energy levels.

Properties
- Determines the level of metabolism and energy in the body
- Protects against toxic effects from radioactive materials
- Helps prevent thyroid disorders
- Acts as a natural antiseptic

NOTES
- Best taken as potassium iodide.
- Take under the supervision of your doctor or nutritionist.
- Iodine is toxic in high doses and may aggravate or cause acne. Large doses may interfere with hormone activity.

Best Sources
Seafood and seaweeds, and most table salt is fortified with iodine

Iron
EU RDA 14 mg
US RDA 10-18 mg (30 mg for pregnant women)
A trace mineral essential for human health. We now know that iron is present in our bodies as haemoglobin, which is the red pigment of blood. Iron is required for muscle protein and is stored in the liver, spleen, bone-marrow and muscles. Iron absorption is highest in childhood, and reduces as we age.

Properties
- Improves physical performance
- Anti-carcinogenic
- Prevents and cures iron-deficiency anaemia
- Improves immunity
- Boosts energy levels

NOTES
- Pregnant, breastfeeding and menstruating women, infants, children, athletes and vegetarians may require increased levels of iron. Iron supplements will be prescribed by your doctor if necessary.

- Excess iron can cause constipation, diarrhoea and rarely, in high doses, death.

Best Sources
Shellfish, brewer's yeast, wheat bran, offal, cocoa powder, dried fruits and cereals

Manganese
EU RDA none
US RDA 2.5-7 mg
An essential trace element necessary for the normal functioning of the brain, and effective in the treatment of many nervous disorders, including Alzheimer's disease and schizophrenia.

Properties
- Maintains a healthy nervous system
- Necessary for normal bone structure
- Important in the formation of thyroxin, in the thyroid gland
- Used in the treatment of some nervous disorders

NOTES
- 2 to 5 mg is considered adequate, but doses up to 10 mg are thought to be safe.

CAUTION
- Toxic levels are usually quite rare, but symptoms of excess manganese may include lethargy, involuntary movements, posture problems and coma.

Best Sources
Cereals, tea, green leaf vegetables, wholemeal bread, pulses and nuts

Magnesium
EU RDA 300 mg
US RDA 300-400 mg
Absolutely essential for every biochemical process in our bodies, including metabolism and the synthesis of nucleic acids and protein.

Properties
- Necessary for many body functions, including energy production and cell replication
- Essential for the transmission of nerve impulses
- Helps to prevent kidney and gallstones
- Useful in treatment of prostate problems
- Repairs and maintains body cells
- Useful in treatment of high blood pressure
- Protects against cardiovascular disease
- Helps to treat PMS

- Dietary intake is thought to be inadequate in the average Western diet.
- High doses are believed to cause flushing of the skin, thirst, low blood pressure and loss of reflexes in some people, although this is rare.

Best Sources
Brown rice, soya beans, nuts, brewer's yeast, whole wheat flour and legumes

Molybdenum
EU RDA none
US RDA 150-500 mcg
An essential trace element and a vital part of the enzyme which is responsible for the utilisation of iron in our bodies. Molybdenum may also be an antioxidant, and recent research indicates that it is necessary for optimum health.

Properties
- Aids in the metabolism of fats and carbohydrates
- Necessary for the excretion of the uric acid from the body
- Protects against cancer
- Prevents anaemia
- Protects against dental caries

NOTES
Molybdenum is toxic in doses higher than 10-15 mg, which cause gout (a build-up of uric acid around the joints).

Best Sources
Wheat, canned beans, wheatgerm, liver, pulses, whole grains, offal and eggs

Phosphorus
EU RDA 800 mg
US RDA 800-1,200 mg
Essential to the structure and function of the body. It is present in the body as phosphates, and in this form aids the process of bone mineralisation and helps to create the structure of the bone.

Properties
- Forms bones and teeth
- Produces energy
- Acts as a co-factor for many enzymes and activates B-complex vitamins
- Increases endurance
- Fights fatigue
- Forms RNA and DNA

Dosage
Phosphorous can be toxic at dosages or intake above 1 g per day, in some cases causing diarrhoea, the calcification of organs and soft tissues, and making the body unable to absorb iron, calcium, magnesium and zinc.
Best Sources
Yeast, dried milk and milk products, wheatgerm, hard cheeses, canned fish, nuts, cereals and eggs

Potassium
EU RDA 3,500 mg
US RDA 900 mg
One of the most important minerals in our bodies, working with sodium and chloride to form 'electrolytes', essential body salts which make up our body fluids. Potassium is crucial for body functioning, playing a role in nerve conduction, our heartbeat, energy production, synthesis of nucleic acids and proteins, and muscle contraction.
Properties
- Activates enzymes which control energy production
- Prevents and treats high blood pressure
- Maintains water balance within cells
- Stabilises internal structure of cells
- Acts with sodium to conduct nerve impulses
NOTES
- In excess doses (above 17 g) potassium may cause muscular weakness and mental apathy, eventually stopping the heart.
Best Sources
Fresh fruit and vegetables, particularly bananas

Selenium
EU RDA 10-75 mcg
US RDA 50-100 mcg
An essential trace element recently recognised as one of the most important nutrients in our diet. It is an antioxidant, and is vitally important in human metabolism.
Properties
- Maintains healthy eyes and eyesight
- Stimulates the immune system
- Improves liver function
- Protects against heart and circulatory diseases
- Can detoxify alcohol, many drugs, smoke and some fats
- Useful in the treatment of arthritis
- Helps treat dandruff

- Protects against a number of cancers

NOTES
- Selenium supplementation should be taken with 30 to 400 IU of vitamin E to ensure that the selenium works most efficiently.
- Selenium can be toxic even in very small doses. Symptoms of excess include blackened fingernails and a garlic-like odour on the breath and skin. Take no more than 500 mcg daily unless supervised by a registered practitioner.

Best Sources
Wheatgerm, bran, tuna fish, onions, tomatoes, broccoli and wholemeal bread

Zinc
EU RDA 15 mg
US RDA 15 mg
One of the most important trace elements in our diet, required for more than 200 enzyme activities within the body.

Properties
- Boosts the immune system
- Crucial in the regulation of our genetic information and for the structure and function of cell membranes
- Prevents and treats colds
- Maintains senses of taste, smell and vision
- Treats acne and other skin problems
- Useful in treatment of rheumatoid arthritis
- Prevents blindness associated with ageing
- Increases male potency and sex drive
- Used in the treatment of infertility

NOTES
- Very high doses (above 150 mg per day) may cause some nausea, vomiting and diarrhoea.

Best Sources
Offal, meat, mushrooms, oysters, eggs, wholegrain products and brewer's yeast

Pyramid Power

Now that you know what you need in your diet on a daily basis, it's time to see how it all goes together.

The pyramid structure works best to show graphically how our diets should be set up. Pin the pyramid on your refrigerator so that you are constantly reminded of the types of foods you should be eating, and in what quantities.

What's a Serving?

Don't worry too much about serving sizes. The main thing is to get the balance right. In other words, if you are eating a variety of different foods, weighted in importance according to the food pyramid, there should be no problem. Half an apple could be considered a fruit serving, for example, as could a glass of orange juice. A handful of nuts or about 75 g of meat would constitute a protein serving, and a slice of wholemeal bread represents one serving of carbohydrates.

Why Fruits and Vegetables?

The importance of fruits and vegetables cannot be over-estimated. A great deal of research has gone into their chemical make-up, and while we know that certain vitamins and minerals they contain have a lot to do with health, we also know that these nutrients don't seem to work as well when they are extracted or synthesised (chemically reproduced). Go for the real thing if you can. Here are some of the reasons why:

● The vitamins, minerals, fibre and protective substances called phytochemicals found in fruits and vegetables help the body to work effectively, and provide the tools it needs to achieve health.

● There is convincing evidence that a diet rich in green leafy vegetables protects against lung and stomach cancers, and probably also against cancer of the mouth and pharynx. Other vegetables, such as broccoli, cauliflower and Brussels sprouts, appear to protect against bowel and thyroid cancer, while Allium vegetables (such as garlic and onions), citrus fruits and tomatoes probably protect against lung, stomach and bladder cancers.

● Fruits and vegetables help to keep body weight under control. Snacking on low-calorie, fibre-rich fruits and vegetables helps keep both calories and hunger in check.

● They maintain cardiovascular health and prevent birth defects. In addition to helping hold the line on body weight, fruits and vegetables are naturally low in sodium, rich in potassium, and virtually fat free.

● Many also provide a healthy dose of folic acid, a vitamin important for preventing neural tube birth defects and keeping levels of a byproduct of protein metabolism called homocysteine under control. Homocysteine is being investigated as a possible independent risk factor for cardiovascular disease.

● A diet rich in fruits and vegetables is associated with a lower risk of strokes, cataracts and a painful bowel disease called diverticulosis, as well as improved blood lipid (fat) levels and a longer, healthier life overall.

Others,
including
sweets,
biscuits,
fast foods
and cakes (not
to be eaten on
a daily basis,
but OK as a very
occasional treat).

Fats and oils, including
butter, olive oil,
unhydrogeneted margarines,
seed and nut oils
(use sparingly).

Proteins, including very lean meats,
fish poultry, cheese, yoghurt, nuts, soya
products (including tofu), pulses such
as lentils, seeds (3 to 5 servings a day).

Fruit and vegetables and their juices. Anything
goes. Remember that the more colourful the
vegetable, the more nutritious it tends to be
(5 to 7 servings a day).

Carbohydrates. Anything wholegrain or unrefined,
including pastas, bread, brown rice, grains, (such as rye,
barley, corn, buckwheat), pulses, potatoes and whole grain
sugar-free cereals (4 to 9 servings a day)

Fluids. Water is the most important. Between 1,000 and 2,00ml
is recommended, depending on age and weather,

Putting It Into Practice

In Part Three of this book we'll look at how best to include these key nutrients in your diet, with a series of plans for people of all ages. In the next part, however, we'll examine the issues surrounding food - this will help you to shop for foods with more confidence, read labels, make choices between the good, bad and downright ugly, and find alternatives to the things you may not want to give up completely.

Part Two
The Issues

There is such a thing as food and such a thing as poison.
But the damage done by those who pass off poison as
food is far less than that done by those who generation
after generation convince people that food is poison.
Paul Goodman (1911-72), US author, poet and critic

Chapter Two

Essential Fats

Low-fat diets are the height of popularity at the moment, and some of the thinking behind this is sound. Saturated fat is unhealthy, and reducing the amount we eat is, as they say, good medicine. It can reduce the risk of stroke, heart problems, overweight and a host of other problems. The problem lies, of course, in the fact that consumers are misled into thinking that *all* fat is bad, and that substituting low-fat versions of the same foods they are accustomed to eating will reduce their weight and the risk of heart disease.

As we discovered in Chapter One, many fats are not only healthy, but essential. Losing all fat from your diet is pretty much an impossibility, but a very low-fat diet can cause problems with your nerves and your ability to assimilate fat-soluble vitamins, and put strain on a number of organs in your body. And when your diet is missing essential fatty acids (EFAs), you can put yourself at risk of a number of health problems.

But the other problem has more to do with our approach to eating than it does to fats in general. We are encouraged to believe that eating low-fat ice cream, snacks, cheeses, biscuits, cakes and ready-made meals in place of their high-fat equivalents is healthy. It is not. People who put themselves on a low-fat diet tend to spend hours reading labels for fat content, and choosing brands that market themselves as being low-, no- or half-fat. The focus is not on healthy eating, but on keeping those fat calories to a minimum. A healthy diet is based around good-quality, nutritious foods, and the majority of low-fat products on the market are anything but. You could, for example, have a diet of low-fat crisps, reduced-fat chocolate, no-fat cakes, all washed down with diet soft drinks. You'd be right in thinking that your fat ratio is lower than it was before, but at what cost? This type of diet offers few if any nutrients, and is much more dangerous in the long run than eating a healthy, balanced diet with full-fat foods.

What's the Answer?

If you focus on eating fresh, wholesome foods, according to the food pyramid (see page 33), exchanging saturated fats for their unsaturated or monounsaturated counterparts, you'll be sure to get the essential fats you need, without the dangers that saturated fats can pose. To be honest, I wouldn't even bother with low-fat foods. They tend to taste inferior, be chemically altered in order to maintain texture and structure (adding to your overall chemical load), and encourage poor eating habits. If you like ice cream, for example, go for a good-quality, delicious and satisfying brand, but just eat a little. You'll feel more satisfied than you would if you ate three fat-free ice cream bars with little taste and a whole host of additives. As long as your diet is healthy, the odd full-fat treat will do no damage. Stick to the 80:20 rule. If 80% of your diet is comprised of healthy foods, then the other 20% can be used as you please.

What Is Essential about Fats?

Saturated and monounsaturated fats provide us with energy, and have a number of roles in the body, but it is the polyunsaturated fats that are the most important. Most of us, however, do not get enough of these fats, and of their components, known as essential fatty acids (EFAs), in our diet.

Basically, EFAs are crucial to a huge number of body functions. In fact, if you take a look at the list of deficiency symptoms below, it's pretty clear that they are an important factor in any healthy diet.

Breaking it Down

Monounsaturated fats (also known Omega-9 fats) are not classed as essential fatty acids, but they can have health benefits. Olive oil, for example, is high in monounsaturated fats, which have been found to lower LDL ('bad') cholesterol and raise HDL ('good') cholesterol, which is one of the factors that contribute to the low rate of heart disease in the Mediterranean.

Polyunsaturated fats can be split into two types:
● Omega-6 oils are found in nuts and seeds, and include evening primrose, starflower and borage oil. These essential fatty acids help prevent blood clots and keep the blood thin. They can also reduce inflammation and pain in the joints, and so are vital in preventing arthritis.
● Omega-3 oils are found in fish oils and linseed (flaxseed) oil and also to some extent in pumpkin seeds, walnuts and dark green vegetables. These oils can help lower blood pressure, reduce the risk of heart disease, soften the skin, increase immune function, increase metabolic rate, improve energy, help with rheumatoid arthritis and alleviate eczema. Oily fish includes mackerel, tuna, sardines, herrings and salmon.

The Department of Health recommends that we should double our intake of Omega-3 oils by eating oily fish two to three times a week. More and more research suggests that it is vital to supplement these fatty acids, and not rely on getting them only in the foods we eat (see page 41).

Most people are deficient in EFAs (both Omega-6 and Omega-3), and take in about three times the saturated fat they should. The balance should be as follows:
No more than one-third of our total fat intake should be saturated (hard) fat
At least one-third should be polyunsaturated fat, providing the Omega oils
The remainder should be monounsaturated (see page 39).
To clarify further, you need about double the quantity of Omega-6 oil as Omega-3 (Omega-3 is more common in our modern diet than Omega-6).

What Do They Do?
Essential fatty acids are converted into substances that keep our blood thin, lower blood pressure, decrease inflammation, improve the function of our nervous and immune systems, help insulin to work, affect our vision, co-ordination and mood, encourage healthy metabolism and maintain the balance of water in our bodies. There's also exciting new research showing that it can affect our children's behaviour and ability to learn.

Choose:
Cold-pressed olive oil for cooking, which does not become unstable when heated.
Add flaxseed oil (available as capsules or as an oil on its own) to your diet. Flaxseed oil has the highest concentration of Omega-3 oils. It shouldn't be heated, but you can drizzle a little in salads or add it to yoghurts or warm foods just before serving. Two or three tablespoons a day is adequate for most adults, and children can get by on one tablespoon.
Remember the daily spoonful of cod liver oil? Our parents and grandparents were not far off the mark. Cod liver oil contains substances that can help to prevent arthritis and other inflammatory conditions. A teaspoon a day for a young child, a tablespoon a day for older children, and 2 tablespoons for adults. Always choose reputable brands who use organic or wild fish sources.
Eat plenty of nuts and seeds.

Fatty Acid Deficiency?

There are some obvious symptoms of fatty acid deficiency. If you suffer from any of the following, the symptoms could be reduced or improved by ensuring that fatty acids are adequately represented in your diet.
Are you particularly prone to infections?

Are you overweight, but not responding to a healthy diet?
Do you suffer from mood swings?
Are you excessively thirsty a lot of the time?
Do you have MS (multiple sclerosis) or diabetes?
Do you suffer from eczema or dry, itching skin?

Do you suffer from any of the following symptoms:
- Aching joints?
- Allergies?
- Arthritis?
- Cracked skin on heels or fingertips?
- Dandruff?
- Depression?
- Difficulty losing weight?
- Dry eyes?
- Dry skin?
- Fatigue?
- Hair loss?
- High blood pressure?
- Irritability?
- Lack of motivation?
- Lifeless hair?
- Painful breasts?
- Poor wound-healing?
- Pre-menstrual syndrome (PMS)?
- Soft or brittle nails?

If more than two or three of these symptoms apply to you, you are likely to have an EFA deficiency.

There are two ways round this. First of all you can take supplements (highly recommended), or you can increase the number of foods that contain EFAs in your diet. A combination of both of these approaches is the ideal solution.

The best EFA supplements are those that contain good quantities of all of the Omega oils, combined in a capsule or liquid form. Drizzle the oil over salads, or sip from a tablespoon. Even flavoured, these oils don't taste particularly nice, but they are worth the momentary discomfort!

The other alternative is to take a daily supplement of linseed (flaxseed) oil, also available in capsule and oil form, for the Omega-3 oils, and evening primrose or borage oils for the Omega-6 oils.

Fat in the Kitchen

The way you cook with and store fats and oils can affect both their nutritional value and their health benefits. In fact, most oils are destabilised by cooking, which makes them not only unhealthy, but potentially carcinogenic (cancer-causing). High temperatures cause oils to oxidise, which generates 'free radicals' in the body (see antioxidants, page 75).

It's important, therefore, to remember the following:

Avoid fried food, and burnt or browned fat. If it burns, or even heats to the point that it vaporises, it's not healthy.

If you do have to fry foods, choose olive oil or butter, which are less prone to oxidation.

Avoid margarines, which are created by hydrogenating vegetable oils. Although the oil is still effectively a polyunsaturate (as all vegetable oils are), the body cannot make use of it. Something called a 'trans-fat' is created, and this type of fat blocks the body's ability to make use of healthy polyunsaturated oils, which contain the EFAs essential to health.

Use only best-quality, cold-pressed vegetable oils. You get what you pay for.

Keep all oils sealed in the fridge, away from heat, light and air. Good-quality oils will go rancid quickly, which means that the health benefits are lost.

Cholesterol

Cholesterol is a fatty substance present in all human cells. A certain amount of cholesterol in the blood is necessary for good health - almost all of this is made in the liver, while the remainder is absorbed from the diet, mainly from meat and dairy products, and egg yolks.

Because cholesterol is a fatty substance, it must be 'packaged' for transportation in the blood. These 'packages' are called lipoproteins, which contain protein and fat, as well as cholesterol. There are several types of lipoproteins, but two of them seem to carry the most significance, especially in terms of heart disease:

1. LDL (low-density lipoprotein) is bad cholesterol - you do not want to have large quantities of it in your blood.
2. HDL (high-density lipoprotein) is good. A third group of fats, called triglycerides, may also be a risk factor for heart disease.

The Good and the Bad

LDL is the 'bad' cholesterol. LDL is mostly made of fat, with a small amount of protein. LDL carries cholesterol from the liver to other parts of the body where it is needed for cell repair and other activities. However, LDL can build up on the walls of the arteries and, over a period of time, this build-up of cholesterol causes the arteries to harden and narrow. This causes reduced blood flow to the body's tissues and the heart muscle (a condition, when it affects the heart, known as *atherosclerosis*). By lowering your LDL intake, you can reduce the risk of atherosclerosis, heart attack, and other complications.

HDL is 'good' cholesterol. It is mostly made up of protein, with just a small amount of fat. HDL helps clear cholesterol from the body by scavenging leftover LDL from the bloodstream and carrying it back to the liver for disposal. If you know or think you are a high risk for heart disease, raising your HDL levels may be beneficial for you, as low HDL is thought to increase the risk of coronary artery disease, while high levels of HDL appear to help protect against the disease.

Cholesterol Tests
Testing for cholesterol is usually just a simple matter of taking a blood sample from a vein and identifying the levels of HDL and LDL. You don't need to alter your diet or fast before you have the test. How often to have your cholesterol levels measured is best determined by your doctor in the light of your family history of heart disease, and there are also home tests available to check levels regularly.

Cholesterol is measured in several ways. The most common way is to measure the number of milligrams of cholesterol per decilitre of blood. Most experts suggest that cholesterol levels for people under 30 should be less than 150 mg/dl. For those over 30, this figure is 180 mg/dl.

How to Lower LDLs and Raise HDLs
- Watch your cholesterol intake carefully. All the cholesterol you require is produced by your body - anything else you eat is surplus to the amount required by your body.
- Lower LDL in your blood by cutting down on animal fats, especially eggs, full-fat cheese and milk, ice cream and butter, while increasing your fibre intake (eating more bran, brown rice, leafy greens), increasing your intake of complex carbohydrates (such as rice, pulses) and losing weight if you are overweight
- Raise HDL in your blood by upping your exercise regime to at least three 20-minute periods of vigorous exercise a week, quitting smoking, losing weight if you are overweight, and balancing your fat intake with 'monounsaturates', which are the good fats that encourage HDL rather than LDL. Good examples of these are olive oil and fish oils. Remarkably, moderate consumption of red wine (about one glass a day) can also increase HDL cholesterol.

The following foods are known to lower cholesterol: apples, bananas, carrots, cold-water fish, dried beans (pulses), garlic, grapefruit and olive oil.

Oats also help to lower cholesterol, and are a good source of fibre, which can help to prevent heart problems.

Essential fatty acids, as found in blackcurrant seed oil, flaxseed oil, borage oil and evening primrose oil, reduce LDL levels and thin the blood.

ChapterThree

Sweet Endings

TheWestern diet has spawned a generation of sugar addicts, and few of us can go for long without something sweet.There is certainly nothing wrong with the odd sweet treat, but most of us get far more sugar than we need in the average diet. In fact, so much sugar is now hidden in unexpected places (baked beans, pasta sauces and soups, for example) that many consumers are genuinely unaware that they are getting as much as they are.

Is Sugar Really a Problem?

It certainly is, and for more reasons than one. Sugar has been viewed as an evil for quite some time now. Not surprisingly, manufacturers have got smart and started calling sugar by its various generic names, including sucrose, glucose, fructose, lactose, galactose and others, in an attempt to put us off the scent.

Some forms of sugar are better than others, however. Those that are more quickly absorbed are the least healthy, because they can make your blood sugar levels soar and plunge (see below).These include glucose and fructose. Obviously the fructose you get from eating a sweet, ripe plum is healthier than the refined versions, but it's sugar nonetheless, and needs to be accounted for when considering your daily intake.

Sugars that are dissolved slightly less quickly are those found in white and brown sugar, honey, and milk. These include sucrose, dextrose, maltose and lactose.When eaten in their natural form, they are less damaging than when they are added to foods and food products.The sugar found in a glass of milk is, for example, largely insignificant on its own, although it does affect blood sugar levels.

Problems arise when too much sugar is taken in, and this normally occurs because so many foods have sugar added to them.

Why Is Sugar So Bad?

First and foremost, sugar has a strong depressive effect on the immune system. According to a 1997 study, as little as six teaspoons a day can reduce the immune response by 25%. Most common foods - particularly those geared towards the fast-food market and children - contain a substantial amount of sugar, which can have a dramatic effect on your health.

Sugar causes blood glucose levels to rise dramatically - causing 'hyperactive' or 'giddy' symptoms. Following the rise there is a dramatic slump, which causes the other set of familiar symptoms - tearfulness, fatigue, mood swings and lack of concentration.

Sugars provide calories and no other nutrients, and they damage tooth enamel, causing decay.

Foods high in sugars (such as biscuits, chocolate bars, cakes, pastries) are also often high in saturated fats, which can lead to overweight, heart disease and even diabetes.

Most importantly, however, the extra calories often displace more nourishing food in the diet. If you fill up on sugary foods, you are less likely to be getting enough vitamins and minerals.

Sugar Content of Common Foods

Food	Number of teaspoons of sugar
1 plain digestive biscuit	½
1 fruit yoghurt	4½
Smarties (1 tube)	7½
1 Mars bar	9½
Tinned sweetcorn (sugar added)	2½
Ketchup (2 tsp)	½
Ice cream (1 scoop)	2
1 bowl sugar-coated cereal	3
1 bowl Cornflakes or Weetabix	trace
1 small can fruit in syrup	10
1 small can fruit in juice	5
1 330-ml can of cola	7
1 113-g package peppermints	20

What's the Answer?

We get far more sugar than we need in even the most healthy diet. The message is to cut out the extras. Don't, for example, be tempted to sweeten cereal or porridge with sugar. If sugar falls within the first three or four ingredients on a particular food's labelling, you can be certain that's a lot. Some sugar-containing foods may surprise you: some muesli bars are made with eight different types of sugar. Be aware that even 'healthy'-sounding foods may be harbouring a lot of sugar!

The best advice is to avoid any foods with added sugar (particularly those that don't need it, like meat, tinned fruits or vegetables, for example), and then cut down on sweet foods. Obviously a chocolate biscuit needs to contain sugar, but look for brands that have 'reduced sugar' content (without any artificial sweeteners added in its place).

What Sweetener?
The odd sweet treat is no sin, and there are some foods that are nicer with a little sweetener. What are pancakes without syrup? Just remember when choosing sweet products, or sweeteners, that some are healthier than others.
- The most natural sweetener used in foods is fruit juice or fruit juice concentrates.
- Dried fruit purees are a healthy choice.
- Molasses and maple syrup are also natural products.
- Date syrup and rice malt syrup can be used as well.

Balancing Blood Sugar

One of the things that a high-sugar diet can cause is a blood sugar problem. This in turn can affect your hormones and a variety of other interlinked systems in the body. Many of us have a blood sugar problem (in other words, an imbalance), and this affects our energy levels and our weight. Given that the majority of us suffer from something called TATT (tired all the time), it will come as no surprise that diet is often its root cause.

When we eat sweet things, the glucose enters our bloodstream quickly. When there is too much, our bodies convert the excess to glycogen (stored in the liver and muscles) and fat. This is done quickly, to avoid excess levels in the blood. A few hours without another sugar fix, and blood sugar levels have dropped. This is when you will feel hungry and experience food cravings, fatigue, palpitations and mood swings, among other things. Then what happens? We feel the need for another sugar boost, or a cup of coffee, which has much the same effect (see caffeine, page 66).

Do you feel exhausted upon rising? Do you need to kickstart your day with a cup of coffee or tea, or a cigarette? Do you need naps during the day, and feel sleepy after meals? Do you feel irritable or faint when you go for more than six hours without eating?

If you can answer yes to any of these questions, it's very likely that your blood sugar levels are unstable, and this is normally caused by dietary factors. There are several ways to deal with this:

- To help maintain a steady blood sugar level during the day, aim to eat complex carbohydrates as part of your main meals, and make sure that you eat little and often during the day. Sometimes just a piece of whole-meal toast can be enough between meals to keep eating urges at bay.
- If you find the symptoms associated with low blood sugar are greatest first thing in the morning, or if you wake during the night with your heart pounding and are unable to get back to sleep, then it is very likely that your blood sugar level has dropped in the night. Eating a small carbohydrate snack such as an oatcake, rice cake or even a bowl of unsweetened cereal, an hour before bed, will help.
- Make sure your complex carbohydrates are unrefined. In general, this means choosing brown instead of white. For example, wholewheat bread, brown rice and wholemeal flour are better than the white versions which have been stripped of essential vitamins, minerals, trace elements and valuable fibre.
- Always dilute pure fruit juices, which can be very high in fructose (fruit sugar).
- Reduce - and preferably avoid - stimulants including tea, coffee, chocolate, canned drinks that contain caffeine, and smoking. These cause the same rises that sugar does.
- Avoid adding sugar to anything you really don't have to.

It's worth noting that diabetes is an extreme form of blood sugar imbalance, and it occurs when our bodies can no longer produce sufficient insulin, a hormone that helps to carry glucose out of the blood and into the cells. The result is too much glucose in the blood and not enough for the cells. Early warning signs of diabetes are similar to those of a blood sugar imbalance, but if diabetes is the problem these warning signs will not go away when you make dietary changes.

What about Artificial Sweeteners?
Unfortunately, these are not the answer. If anything, they are worse than sugar in terms of their impact on the body. They may help you cut down on calories, and possibly tooth decay, but they are potentially dangerous. Saccharine is linked to cancer in rats, while aspartame has been linked with the growth of malignant brain tumours. Researchers from King's College in London are investigating the links in a three-year study. Aspartame is 200 times sweeter than sugar, and it is used in many low-calorie and no-calorie drinks, as an additive in foods, and as a sweetener for hot drinks such as tea and coffee. Apart from obvious cancer fears, adults have reported dizziness, headaches, epileptic-like seizures and menstrual problems after consuming aspartame.

The Bottom Line

The real answer is to learn to enjoy naturally sweet foods such as fruit and some vegetables, focusing on the fresh and whole, rather than on processed foods or junk. If you feel the need for a sweet after dinner, try some fresh fruit with yoghurt instead, or go for a fruit crumble with as little added sugar as possible. Everything you do to reduce the sugar in your diet will have a positive impact on your health and that of your family. You will find that your energy levels improve and that your weight stabilises as your blood sugar comes under control. You'll also be much less likely to suffer from chronic colds or other viruses, and more likely to get a clean bill of health from your dentist.

Chapter Four

What's in Our Food?

If you took heed of everything you read in the paper about the food we eat, you'd be living on rice cakes (and even those can contain genetically modified ingredients!). The answer is not a perpetual fast, but a sensible approach to eating based on a clear understanding of the issues.

Mad Cows and Meat

BSE, Bovine Spongiform Encephalopathy, is a degenerative brain disease in cattle. CJD stands for Creitzfeldt-Jakob disease, named after the two men who discovered it. This condition is also a degenerative brain disease, which usually affected elderly people. In 1996 scientists confirmed a strain or variant of the disease among young people, which they have until now referred to as nvCJD (new variant CJD). This disease is now known just as vCJD, the 'n' having been dropped because it is no longer new.

There is no cure for vCJD, which causes holes in the brain and a host of physical and mental symptoms including depression, blurred vision, slurred speech, sometimes aggressiveness, followed by loss of control of the limbs, and eventually of the entire body.

The 1980s saw the biggest ever epidemic of BSE in cattle, and vCJD emerged shortly thereafter in humans. The link was made when it was discovered that most vCJD victims lived in the UK, where the cattle epidemic took place. Scientists believe that the most likely cause of vCJD in humans was the consumption of BSE-infected beef between the years 1986 and 1989, when contaminated meat was likely to have been prevalent in the food chain.

The origins of BSE are not entirely clear, but it is believed that its spread coincided with new feeding practices, where the remains of other cattle - and perhaps even of sheep and other animals - were processed and fed to cattle.

There are doubts about whether or not there will be a mass epidemic of vCJD. Since 1995, 48 people in the UK have died of the disease; 17 died in 1998; the figures for 1999 are unconfirmed at 9 deaths. But because the disease can incubate for 10 to 15 years, it's difficult to know how many will be affected. The result? Beef was off the shopping list for many forsome time, British beef on the bone was banned, and only recently has it been declared completely safe to eat.

Is It Safe?
In the UK the government arranged for the mass slaughter of millions of cattle at risk of infection, and only young cattle were allowed into the food chain. All young cattle are now traced from birth to death to prove they are free of the disease, and they are issued with 'passports' and tagged in the ear. Scientists believe that any future cases will be in people who are already incubating the disease. The chances of newly acquiring the disease are now very remote.

So, according to the majority of research, we have nothing to worry about on the BSE front. There are other issues affecting meat, though.

Hormones in Meat
European Union farmers are banned from giving hormones to cattle because of health fears, but in the US, natural and synthetic hormones are routinely given to cattle to boost the amount of quality meat they produce without having to feed them more. The female sex hormones oestrogen and progesterone stimulate extra muscle and fat, while the male sex hormone testosterone increases muscle growth and decreases fat production.

Alarmingly, oestrogen has been linked to breast cancer in women, and to infertility in men. Progesterone may increase the development of several 'female' cancers, including ovarian, breast and uterine, while testosterone is linked to prostate cancer in men.

The synthetic chemical stilboestrol, which is similar to the chemicals fed or injected into cattle in the US, was used in the EU until a ban on treating meat with hormones was introduced in 1988. This led to reports of children growing breasts early after eating contaminated food. Furthermore, evidence supports the idea that even small residues of oestradiol (a naturally occurring oestrogen) in meat may produce tumours.

The EU Scientific Committee for Veterinary Measures has warned that all sex hormones used in the US could pose a risk of cancer, genetic problems and brain disease, and claims that children are most at risk.

Is It Safe?
The concerns and associated risks mean it is not safe to eat meat that has been injected with hormones. Because of the ban in the EU, Europeans obviously have a reduced risk. Nor are travellers to the US likely to be affected to any large degree, because the hormones need to build up before they have an effect. However, to be on the safe side, avoid eating any US meat products (including stock cubes and gelatine), unless they are reared organically (see page 63), until studies can show that they are completely safe. There is a raging debate between the US and the EU, and the chances are that hormones may be reintroduced even here in the EU at

some stage. Watch out for them, and avoid all but organic meat products if the US wins this fight.

Antibiotics in Meat
Intensive farming methods have ensured that most animals are raised in small spaces, under stressful conditions. These conditions are a breeding ground for disease - and may in fact have contributed to the increase in Salmonella and E-coli infections in humans. (An estimated 60% of chickens sold in the US are infected with Salmonella, and that figure may be as high as 75% in the EU.) To combat the problem, animals are routinely given antibiotics. These protect the animals against disease and also encourage them to grow faster. The majority of pigs and poultry reared in the West are given antibiotics with their feed or water.

Are They Safe?
No. When we eat foods containing high levels of antibiotics, we run the risk of developing a resistance to them. The spread of antibiotic resistance could mean that some of the antibiotics used in human medicine become less effective or, in extreme cases, completely ineffective. For example, in the US one of the best drugs for treating typhoid had to be banned because its over-use in animals had rendered it useless in humans.

Once again, organic meat and poultry are guaranteed to be free of antibiotics. To be on the safe side, children in particular should, as much as possible, be given nothing but. Because we do not know the long-term effects of our new ways of producing foods, it is much safer to take no risks. We don't need a lot of meat (see page 14), so although organic produce is still more expensive, the investment could save your life.

BST
One of the reasons dairy cows produce milk is a hormone called BST (bovine somatotropin), which is naturally produced by their bodies. Typically, when something works we want more of it, whether it's natural or not. Genetic engineers have come up with a BST injection that encourages cows to produce more milk - up to 20% more in fact.

In the US this hormone has been legal since 1994. It was banned in the EU, and in Canada, following some disturbing tests and studies, but the ban has been under review, and it looks like a battle that the EU may lose.

Is It Safe?
Obviously not. Some farmers using BST are finding that disease levels are rising in their herds. Among the problems: more cases of mastitis, lowered fertility, lameness and heat stress. The long-term effects are as yet

unknown. Veterinary experts claim that the hormone exhausts the cows to such an extent that they become more susceptible to infection, which means more antibiotics.

If BST is reintroduced to the EU, organic milk is the only answer. Not just because of the as yet unknown long-term effects of BST on humans, but because of the dangers of this increased use of antibiotics.

Barbecues

When we barbecue or chargrill food, fat drips on to the coals. Some of this is not completely combusted, and it forms a smoke which contains carcinogens (benzopyrene), which is then deposited on the food. Furthermore, charring protein-rich foods (such as meat) may result in the production of mutagenic (cell structure-changing) and carcinogenic (cancer-causing) substances.

Is It Safe?

Sadly, no. Several studies show that the risk of cancer is greatly increased in people who eat a lot of charred or fried foods. If a BBQ is an odd treat, don't worry too much, but if it is the mainstay of your summer diet, think again. Burnt sausages, burgers (or any other source of protein), whether they burned while being grilled, fried or barbecued, hold some potential risks, so avoid them where possible.

Nitrates

These are chemicals widely used as preservatives for meat and meat products such as bacon, ham and salami (and almost every smoked meat). Even bigger sources of nitrates are found in vegetables grown with nitrate fertilisers - for example, spinach and beets - and in drinking water in areas where these fertilisers are heavily used.

Are They Safe?

Absolutely not. In food, nitrates appear in fairly minimal quantities, and most healthy people will be able to 'detoxify' fairly easily. However, someone who eats lots of meat, salami, hot dogs, bacon and even smoked chicken, fish or beef will be at higher risk. What are the risks? First and foremost, nitrates convert to substances which are known to be carcinogenic. Nitrates are also implicated in 'blue baby' syndrome in new-born infants. In rural areas where nitrate levels in water are up to four times higher than national averages, childhood diabetes appears to be 25% more common.

Avoid any nitrate-containing foods to ensure that you aren't increasing your cancer risk. For the average person the odd piece of bacon at breakfast or in pasta, or the occasional ham sandwich should not cause undue problems. Choose unsmoked bacon, if possible, as this will reduce your exposure to at least one of the cancer-causing chemicals. If nitrate-rich foods are the mainstay of your diet, it's time to make changes.

Genetically Modified (GM) Foods

This is a tricky one. GM foods have not been proved conclusively to cause damage to health, but the public is concerned enough to have demanded that they be adequately labelled and, in many cases, withdrawn.

Genetic modification involves isolating and identifying a gene that produces a desired characteristic. This gene is copied, then inserted into another species. The idea is that the very best aspects of plants (or even animals and humans!) can be fitted together like a jigsaw to produce the ideal product. For example, scientists have produced tomatoes that don't rot, insect-proof corn and potatoes, and a host of other goodies, the best known of which is the herbicide-resistant soya bean, so that soya plants (which are particularly susceptible to herbicides) could be sprayed, leaving the surrounding weeds dead but the soya bean plants unharmed. Soya beans are processed into oil and flour - and then used in 60% of processed foods, including cooking oils, margarines, salad dressings, sauces, bread, biscuits, cakes, pizzas, noodles, ice creams and alternatives to dairy products such as tofu, tempeh and miso.

Are They Safe?
The answer is that we don't know for sure. Between 70% and 90% of us are against genetically engineering or modifying food on the basis that it isn't doing us any real good, and for the following reasons:

- The British consumer is fed up with food issues. We weren't warned about beef and BSE until it was too late. GM foods were yet another case of the government saying 'We are sure it's safe', but this time the public didn't let them get away with it. GM foods are now labelled in the UK and we can choose not to buy them.
- An increasing number of us suffer from allergies, and that number is growing all the time. Allergies are often caused by proteins, and genetic engineering results in new proteins in food products. GM foods could trigger allergic reactions (some serious enough to cause death), or they could encourage susceptibility to more allergens. Again, we don't know for sure.
- Julia Hales and John Elkington, author of *Manual 2000*, raise another concern about the 'marker' genes used by scientists to see whether a desired gene has been incorporated into an organism. The rot-free

tomato, for example, can survive otherwise lethal doses of antibiotics. Antibiotics may not harm plants, but there is concern that antibiotic resistance may spread to other species. In theory, at least, this may already be possible via the intestines of animals fed unprocessed genetically engineered maize. Companies have been made aware of this problem and have agreed to use alternatives in the future.

- GM foods don't focus on nutrition, and there is a real worry that we may end up with beautiful, quick-growing plants that have no nutritional value.
- All plants contain their own toxins, which our bodies deal with adequately. We don't know what genetic modification will do to toxins in plants, and there is a very real concern that they could raise them to unacceptable levels, or alter them so that they become much more dangerous.
- GM foods have not been thoroughly tested for their long-term effects.
- *We* don't benefit from GM foods; manufacturers and producers do. It's always wise to be concerned where big money is at stake for manufacturers. They have a vested interest in convincing us these foods are safe to buy, even if they can't prove it.
- GM foods could destroy our natural environment. Any mistakes are out there, transferred by pollen, animals, birds, water etc. and can't be reversed. We could be breeding super-pests by creating plants that are pest-resistant or antibiotic - resistant; we are altering the very structure of plants at top speed, and without anywhere near adequate testing. Even organic foods can be affected if they are, for example, downwind from a GM farm. The ramifications of that could be massive.

In short, too much is unknown. GM foods are not natural and they have the potential to cause harm. Avoid GM products wherever possible (and that's not always easy). Organic food is GM free (and will hopefully stay that way). Eat organic whenever possible, or look for labels that state 'GM-free'. The number of GM-free products is increasing all the time.

Foods Likely to Contain GM Ingredients
Always read the label. Many manufacturers are taking great pains to remove GM ingredients from their products. If it says GM-free, it is.

Reduced-fat and 'light' foods
Processed foods from the US (where genetic modification is worth billions of dollars every year, and where no restraints or labelling practices are in place)
Ready-prepared sandwiches and meals

Anything containing soya or soya milk (including tofu)
Prepared pasta and noodles
Burgers, meatloaf, sausages, sausage rolls, pies, pastries and quiche
Cooked sliced meats
Cooking oils, margarines and spreads
Frozen yoghurts, ice cream and other desserts
Biscuits, cakes, chocolate, sweets
Flavoured yoghurts
Processed meat, fish, poultry or vegetarian foods, such as fish fingers, veggie burgers and chicken nuggets
Store-bought (and usually takeaway) pizzas
Cheese - hard, soft and processed
Mayonnaise, sauces and dips
Dried fruits
Crisps, tortilla chips, popcorn
Tinned and packet soups
Soft drinks, hot chocolate and some coffees
Does that cover a good portion of your weekly shopping list? You can see why there is concern.

Food Irradiation

Irradiation is a fairly new technology which involves exposing food to high doses of radiation in order to kill insects and pests, reduce levels of bacteria like Salmonella and Listeria, delay ripening and rotting, so that foods can be kept for longer, and completely sterilise foods, which is a bonus for anyone with a weakened or immature immune system such as the chronically or terminally ill, babies and the elderly.

Is It Safe?
Because it is a relatively new science, the dangers are as yet unknown. We do know that irradiation can substantially reduce the nutritional content of foods - by up to 90%. So the food may look better, taste better and last longer, but it will have very little nutritional value - the main reason for eating it. Studies show that irradiation may also leave some active bacteria.

Irradiated foods are not labelled at present, so it's virtually impossible to distinguish them from non-irradiated ones. Organic foods are not irradiated, so they are the safest option (see page 63) until we know more.

Pesticides

Pesticides are commonly sprayed to kill pests, but they play a dual role of contaminating the plants and the surrounding area, as well as the healthy animals and insects who would have eaten the pests in the natural order of things.

Are They Safe?
Pesticides can damage our immune systems, making us more vulnerable to illness and disease. The immune systems of other animals are also affected. For example, a plague that was killing dolphins turned out to be caused by a common virus to which they would normally have been resistant. Blood samples showed that they had high levels of pesticides in their bodies. Other symptoms, in both animals and humans, include fertility problems.

Much of the food that we eat contains measurable quantities of pesticide residues, even though the chemicals have been applied legally. Some imported foods may even contain residues of pesticides banned here in the UK. Given that we are encouraged to eat lots of fruits and vegetables, the potential exposure is a matter of real concern.

Among the most controversial pesticides in recent years have been organophosphates. Their effects are believed to include: nervous system problems, with early symptoms including: headaches, excessive sweating, breathing difficulty, vomiting, blurred vision, slurred speech, slow thinking and loss of memory. Later come convulsions, coma and even - in extreme circumstances - death. Organophosphates are commonly used on a variety of fruits and vegetables, including bananas and carrots.

Here's some more compelling research:
- The World Health Organization has estimated that between 3.5 and 5 million people globally suffer acute pesticide poisoning every year. A Danish study claims that some pesticides, found throughout the whole food chain, can lead to breast cancer.
- 40% of pesticides now in use have been proved to be cancer-promoting and linked to birth defects or decreased fertility in men and women.
- Pesticide exposure is associated with depression, memory decline, destabilisation of moods, rhinitis, asthma, eczema, migraine, irritable bowel syndrome, Parkinson's disease and cancer.
- Pesticide use is on the increase. At present, 400 million litres of pesticides and herbicides are sprayed on to food and pastures in the UK. It's ludicrous to think that a product designed to kill another living organism could have no effect whatsoever on our bodies.

To be healthy, all of us need fruits and vegetables, carbohydrates, fats and proteins. The benefits of these foods outweigh (although perhaps only marginally) the problems associated with pesticides. If you can afford it, go organic (see page 63).

Additives, Preservatives and Other Chemicals

Not only are food additives a major cause of health problems, but they can affect growth, mood, concentration, sleeping patterns and overall resistance to infection by overloading our systems with toxins. Children's food is full of some of the worst additives, largely because manufacturers (rightly) believe that something brightly coloured, over-sweetened and refined and processed to look like your child's favourite cartoon character is more likely to appeal to a faddy eater. As boring as it may sound, learn to read labels, and take some time to educate yourself about this problem.

Every food contains natural chemicals, while many other chemicals added to foods make them safer for us to eat. Some chemicals change the consistency of a product, others make it last longer, and still others give it flavour or colour. Vitamins and minerals are often added to foods to make them more nutritious. How do you separate the good from the bad?

E-numbers

E-numbers are food additives that have been cleared for use in Europe. Officially, foods contain too little of them to do us any harm. Some are in fact good for us, such as E300, which is simply vitamin C. Others are preservatives which are needed if the product is to survive for any length of time.

Many manufacturers have cottoned on to the fact that people are wary of E-numbers, and have begun putting the full name of the chemical instead of its E-number on labelling. Longer names are bound to confuse the consumer, so beware of long lists of unusual looking words, particularly in foods that are brightly coloured, highly flavoured or very sweet. Watch out particularly for *tartrazine*, or E102, which is a yellow food colouring that is now believed to cause hyperactivity, especially in children. Also on the danger list are *amaranth* and *erythrosien* (red colours, E123 and E127), which are possibly carcinogens.

What to Look For
- The main E-numbers linked with health problems include: E102, E110, E122, E123, E124, E127, E129, E131, E133, E142, E150C, E151, E153, E154, E155, E210-E224, E226, E227, E228, E232, E249, E250, E251, E252, E284, E285, E320, E321, E512, E533B, E621, E942, E954, E1440.
- Healthy, antioxidant E-numbers include from E300 to E304 (vitamin C), and E307 to E309 (vitamin E).
- E310 to E312, E320 and E321 may be dangerous to asthmatics and to

people who are sensitive to aspirin. They are also among the additives that are forbidden in baby foods.

- E249 to E252 are nitrates, usually found in cured meats such as bacon and ham. However, they do also protect against botulism, which is the most toxic poison known.
- E621, MSG, is used to enhance meaty or savoury flavours. Some people are sensitive to large quantities. It can cause headaches, giddiness, nausea, muscle pains and heart palpitations.

The British Nutrition Foundation believes that more research is necessary before we can establish that additives are safe, particularly in the light of the number of reported allergic reactions.

Labels

Reading every label of every food you buy would mean spending a day a week in the supermarket, but it's a good idea to read the odd label - you might be surprised by what you find. Many of the foods that we consider to be healthy simply are not. They've got so many things added to them that they've become chemical cocktails.

All additives are rigorously tested to ensure that they fall within safety limits. The problem is that all of us tend to eat a lot of the things we like. A high intake of any particular additive could take us well above acceptable levels. Nor has there been any research into the combinations of chemicals, and while they may be 'safe' in small dosages or singly, we don't know what they might do when they are taken together. Finally, we need to ask ourselves what 'safe' really means. If something causes illness or death when taken in large doses, is it really all right to have it in moderation? I think the answer is no.

Let's look at some of the various additives in detail:

FLAVOURS
Unless the flavour is preceded by the word 'natural', it's a synthesised chemical, and it's worth avoiding. 'Natural-identical' flavours are not natural. Don't be fooled. Flavours do not have E-numbers and they are not normally listed on food products because they would reveal the 'secret recipe' of the product.

EMULSIFIERS
These are used to prevent ingredients from separating (for example, oil and vinegar). Emulsifiers are considered largely benign, but it's worth watching for problems. Many emulsifiers are synthetic, and may contribute to toxic overload.

STIMULANTS

Many drinks and some foods contain stimulants, the most common being caffeine. Apart from tea and coffee, caffeine is found in cola drinks, chocolate, and even headache tablets. Caffeine excites the brain by stimulating the heart and circulation, and by increasing adrenaline levels. It would be difficult to get enough in food or drink to cause death, but stimulants like caffeine are not recommended for children in any quantity. They can cause digestive problems, headaches, anxiety and depression, and they may interfere with crucial stages of development.

COLOURS

Food manufacturers have backtracked on this one. At one time all sorts of foods were filled with extra, artificial colours, but these were the first to be implicated in food-additive scares and manufacturers have taken note. You can now find many products without 'artificial colours', and you should seek them out.

Some of the colourings that should definitely be avoided are: E100, E102, E104, E107, E110, E120, E122, E123, E124, E127, E128, E131, E132, E133, E142, E150, E151, E153, E154 and E180. For the record, they cover most colours in the rainbow.

STABILISERS

These improve the texture of foods. Many are natural, such as lecithin. Again, there is no direct link between stabilisers and ill-health, although E407 (carrageen) has been put on the additive hit-list by various authorities.

FILLERS

These are substances added to products to absorb water and thicken and bulk them out. These are empty calories with few if any nutrients. Avoid them if you can. Fillers include: cornflour, rice flour, soya flour, gelatine, pectin, vegetable gums and various types of starch. Are they dangerous? Perhaps. A 1998 study showed that modified starch (which is cornflour that has been chemically treated) caused loose stools in infants. That may not seem significant, but any diarrhoea in infants can lead to dehydration fairly quickly, and to loss of nutrients that are essential for growth.

PRESERVATIVES

There's no question that preservatives play an important role, as most foods would go off rapidly without them, and potentially deadly diseases such as botulism can be prevented by their (prudent) use. There are, however, some that have been associated with health problems, and worsen symptoms of complaints such as asthma. The E-numbers in question include: E210-213 (some of which are linked with gastric irritation and problems with conception, among other things), E220-223, E227, E230, E231, E232, E239, and E249-252.

SWEETENERS
(See page 47).

FLAVOUR ENHANCERS
The big one is MSG or E621. Used in a variety of products, including Chinese food, sauces, and a wide range of ready-prepared meals, MSG has been shown to over-excite - even kill - brain cells. Given the potential risks to children, baby food manufacturers have been forced, by law, to stop adding it to their products.

ANTIOXIDANTS
These are not the same thing as the antioxidants we take for health (see page 75). These chemicals prevent damage to food products caused by air. Watch out for E310, E311, E312, E320 and E321. These should not be consumed.

VITAMINS AND MINERALS
Good news if you have an unhealthy diet, but don't be fooled by unhealthy products with added nutrients. Adding vitamins to a fizzy drink does not make it healthy. In fact, the chemicals contained in it far outweigh any benefits that the nutrients might offer.

So Are They Safe?
Avoid additives as much as possible. Some are necessary to keep food fresher and to make it last longer, but you'll be much better off serving fresh, natural foods, both to keep the toxin levels down and to prevent reactions that can cause ill-health.

Food Poisoning

In the UK, food poisoning incidents have increased by 400% in just 10 years. While there are no documented cases of organic meat or poultry setting off food poisoning epidemics, contaminated feed and diseased animals are commonplace in industrial agriculture. According to government statistics, most non-organic beef cattle are contaminated with e-Coli 0157:H7; over 90% of chickens are tainted with campylobacter, and 30% of poultry are infected with salmonella.

Foods commonly affected include meats of most types, poultry, ready-prepared meals, prewashed vegetables and salads, cheeses and, indeed, anything that is past its sell-by date.

Is It Safe?

Most food-borne illnesses are destroyed by cooking foods at high temperatures, and, in the case of vegetables, by washing scrupulously in a mild detergent especially designed for washing fruits and vegetables. If you take steps to avoid or prevent the risks, you are a lot less likely to suffer from food poisoning. High-risk groups - such as children, the elderly, pregnant women and anyone with a serious illness or immune problem - should avoid eating the danger foods, to be on the safe side.

Food Safety

- Fruits and vegetables should look fresh and undamaged. Leaves should be crisp, root vegetables firm, with the skin unbroken. Fruits like melons should smell ripe but not too sweet, and should be firm to the touch.
- Tinned foods should be in an intact tin, with no bulges, rust marks or dents. Any damage may have allowed bacteria or other germs to enter the tin.
- Pay attention to the 'best-before' and 'use-by' dates. You can probably safely go a day after most of these dates, but remember that food is at its best when it is fresh. Every day past a sell-by date means a reduction in nutritional value. You also run the risk of food poisoning.
- Ready-prepared salads and pre-chopped vegetables are inferior to their fresh, uncut counterparts, but if you don't have time for much food preparation, and are unlikely to eat anything fresh unless it is prepared for you, then these are a good buy. Watch out, however, for any signs of age, such as browning lettuce, dried-out vegetables, and excess moisture in the package. Always wash even those that claim to be 'ready to eat'.
- Frozen foods should be at freezing temperature, and kept that way, to maintain their freshness and to ensure that they do not become contaminated. Choose packages from the bottom of the freezer (checking dates), and save your freezer shopping till last, so that you have an opportunity to get them home before they defrost.
- Open egg cartons to check that the eggs are not dirty or cracked. If there is any 'fur' on the eggs, they may be mouldy.
- Raw meat should look firm, fresh and a healthy pink or red colour. Anything greying or bleached-looking is not recommended for eating. Ensure that raw and cooked products do not come into contact with

each other. Choose simple cuts of meat rather than products made with mixed meat, which are at greater risk of cross-contamination. Avoid ready-to-eat chickens that do not require cooking. These chickens are one of the major causes of food poisoning in the UK.

When choosing fish, don't buy anything that smells strongly. Don't freeze fresh fish: eat it the same day that it is purchased. When buying fresh, look for clear eyes, red gills, shiny skin and scales in place. The fish should feel firm and slightly resilient if you press it. Avoid fish with dull eyes or slimy skin.

The Organic Solution

In a world with a bewildering array of problems associated with food, it's not surprising that consumers are choosing to vote with their feet - and head off in the direction of a type of food production that pretty much eliminates the risks. The answer for so many consumers is organic food, which has environmental and economic benefits, as well as those associated with health.

All organic foods conform to these specifications:

- They are grown under natural conditions without the use of chemicals.
- Organic vegetables are grown without artificial fertilisers or pesticides, in ground that has been tested and declared free of contamination. This prevents the practice of intensive farming, where land is artificially fertilised to produce the greatest number of crops.
- Nothing labelled 'organic' is irradiated, or contains genetically modified organisms.
- Choosing organic food means avoiding all of the hundreds of additives or E numbers regularly found in conventional foods.
- Organically raised animals are given comfortable surroundings, and fed food that has been organically produced. Land used for grazing must not have pesticides or any other chemicals sprayed on it.
- No antibiotics or other drugs are given to organically raised animals, unless they are genuinely ill. If drugs are required, the animals are not slaughtered for some time, to avoid any residue being left in the animals' system, which may eventually reach our plates.
- They are not fed anything containing animal products, if they are natural herbivores, and most of their food is found in their natural environment - the fields of the farm.
- Organically raised animals are 'free-range', which means that they can wander outdoors instead of living their lives in a stable or cage.

Organic on a Budget

The benefits are fairly clear, but the sticking point is, of course, the price. Organic food costs more, and for good reason. Organic food costs more to produce because much of the work is done by hand and on smaller farms, meaning lower yields and higher production costs. But you get what you pay for, and for many consumers, it's worth the money.

However, not everyone can afford an entirely organic diet, and not everything is available in organic form. If your budget doesn't stretch as far as you would like, try at least to choose organic when it comes to the following products:

- Baby food
- Strawberries, peaches, apples and bananas
- Rice, oats and other grains
- Milk
- Corn and green beans

Pesticide contamination in the non-organic equivalents is quite unacceptable, sometimes as high as 65%! In general, if you tend to eat a lot of a specific food, such as bread or apples, for example, try to buy organic brands or products. It will make a difference in the long run. Even if you can't afford much more than this, you'll be taking a step in the right direction.

Chapter Five

Healthy Drinking

What we drink is just as important as the food we choose to eat. Good drinking habits will enhance a healthy diet, and help to make up for a poor one. And drinking unhealthily can undo a lot of the good that a healthy diet offers. Drinks take up a good proportion of the supermarket aisles, and there's no question that we need to drink to stay alive!

But the apparently limitless choices can be mind-boggling, and it's often difficult to know whether a drink is healthy or downright unsafe. Here's a guide to the liquid maze!

Water

The importance of water was discussed in Chapter One, and it's fairly obvious why we need it. In the West we take a clean water supply for granted, and water is the mainstay of the majority of drinks we consume throughout the day. Without water our cells cannot build new tissue efficiently, toxic products build up in our bloodstream, and our blood volume decreases so that we have less oxygen and nutrients transported to our cells, all of which can leave us weak, tired and at risk of illness.

The Best Waters
- Bottled natural mineral water is the best bet. If you drink bottled water, look for one with low sodium (lower than 20 mg of sodium per litre) and the weakest mineral concentration, to be on the safe side. Bottled natural mineral water is guaranteed to be free of all traces of pollution, and it is naturally free of bacteria.
- Bottled spring water is a waste of money. There are fewer regulations governing these types of waters, and there have even been reports of tap water being bottled and sold as spring water.
- If your budget doesn't stretch to bottled water, or you find transporting the bottles from the supermarket too cumbersome, the next best option is filtered water. There are various types of filters, and you'll have to shop carefully to ensure that you are getting what you want. Unfortunately, this is another case where you get what you pay for. A plumbed-in filtering system is ultimately the most effective at removing unwanted pollutants and other chemicals, but again, it might be

unaffordable. Most 'jug' filters remove only chlorine and floating particles, although there are some new ones on the market that claim to remove bacteria, pesticides, industrial chemicals and heavy metals. Always change your filter regularly, as they become useless - and a breeding ground for bacteria - if used too long.

Coffee or Tea?

Probably the most popular drinks with adults, the bad news is that both contain toxins and can be unhealthy in large amounts. But it's important to be realistic about this one. The odd cup of coffee is unlikely to do any harm, and tea is now known to have a whole range of health benefits which will probably outweigh the risks.

One of the best known toxins that occurs in both coffee and tea is caffeine. For the record, tea contains about 60% of the caffeine of coffee, and chocolate contains about the same. Caffeine stimulates the brain, which helps to keep us awake and thinking clearly, hence its appeal. But there is a downside to all this. Caffeine has a diuretic effect on the body and so depletes valuable stores of vitamins and minerals that are essential for a healthy hormone balance. Caffeine in tea, coffee, chocolate, and caffeinated soft drinks are all stimulants and cause a fast rise in blood sugar followed by a quick drop, which contributes to the roller-coaster ride of blood sugar swings (see page 47).

Both tea and coffee reduce the absorption of iron and zinc; therefore, any coffee and tea you drink would be best taken between meals rather than with meals. The best advice is to keep caffeine to a minimum, perhaps just a cup or two a day. But eliminate it gradually! Suddenly giving up coffee, for example, can cause a variety of unpleasant withdrawal symptoms, such as headaches, shaking and muscle cramps. If you do drink a little too much, make sure you drink plenty of fresh water to help cleanse your system.

Decaffeinated coffee may be lower in caffeine, but it is not any better for you. Indeed, some processes of decaffeinating actually increases the chemical content, making it a stronger toxin.

Tea does have some health-giving properties, and as long as you don't drink it too strong it should be lower in caffeine than coffee. Black tea contains chemicals that are believed to help prevent some forms of heart disease. Scientists have also discovered that compounds found in black tea may attack harmful bacteria in the mouth which cause gum disease and cavities. Green tea is believed to improve resistance to stomach and skin cancers, and to stimulate the immune system. As long as you don't load it with sugar and milk, and keep your intake to a minimum, it looks like tea can stay on the menu!

Herbal Teas and Tisanes

The healthy properties of herbal teas and tisanes are well known. They act to cleanse and strengthen the body, and have a wide range of therapeutic benefits. They also do not have the irritant effects of tea and coffee, and do not normally contain any caffeine. Here are some of the best teas to try for various ailments:

Calming the nerves, inducing sleep	*Chamomile, limeflower, passion flower, red clover*
Infections or colds	*Rosehip, comfrey, aniseed, licorice, sage*
To improve liver function	*Agrimony, mugwort, angelica*
Indigestion or tummyache	*Peppermint, dill, fennel, lemongrass, aniseed, lemon balm*
As a tonic	*Nettle, mint, ginseng, rosemary, raspberry and strawberry leaf*
Diuretics for weight loss and the kidneys	*Celery seed, dandelion, couchgrass, golden rod, agrimony*

You can also drink herbal teas for their flavour alone. Delicious blends are now available from most supermarkets and healthfood shops. Try them iced in summer: iced peppermint tea with lemon and fresh mint is a delicious option.

Alcohol

This is a dubious one. There's no question that alcohol is an important part of our culture; in fact, meeting for a drink is one of our favourite social activities. Once again, in moderation, alcohol will not harm, and it may even enhance your health. The problem is, of course, that too much can be harmful, and many people are over-drinking.

It doesn't take much alcohol to start the downward spiral. People who regularly drink a bottle of wine a day (which is easy when you have a drink at lunchtime, a few drinks with friends after work, and some wine with dinner) will experience liver damage, nutritional deficiency (alcohol robs the body of B vitamins in particular), brain shrinkage and a host of other conditions, including digestive problems and impaired memory. Fertility is also affected by drinking. Women drinking three or more drinks a day have an increased risk of breast cancer. Alcohol is also full of calories, which can make a difference if you are trying to keep your weight stable.

The Unit System
Experts recommend that women drink no more than 14 units a week, and men no more than 21. One unit of drink is a half-pint of average strength beer (about 4%), or a single of 70-proof spirit, or one glass of wine.
The main problem is that alcohol makes you feel good. One or two drinks cause a feeling of relaxation and a mild sensation of euphoria. Shy people feel more confident, and it is, for most people, easier to socialise with one or two drinks inside us. But after only three or four drinks we will experience reduced co-ordination, hampered speech, slow reaction time, decreased inhibitions and impaired judgement.

Not All Doom and Gloom
If you rarely overindulge and seldom have a hangover but you do sip a couple of soothing glasses of wine at the end of the day, the chances are you will live longer and experience a better quality of life. One or two glasses (units) of alcohol a day relieves stress, helps you think more clearly, fends off heart disease and promotes longevity. In fact, death rates for people who savour a drink a day are 16% lower than for people who either drink more or nothing at all.

Red wine in particular seems to be of value. Grapes contain an antioxidant called 'resveratrol' which decreases the 'stickiness' of the blood platelets and keeps blood vessels from narrowing.

The answer is to drink infrequently and to take breaks from time to time, to give your liver a chance to recover and renew. Stick to your weekly unit recommendation, and if you have a choice, go for the red.

Soft Drinks

Fizzy Drinks
The majority of fizzy drinks contain nothing but artificial sweeteners, flavours, sugar, caffeine and water. Some fizzy drinks contain a little fruit juice (watch for the percentage), but not normally enough to make these drinks worthwhile. Even fizzy mineral water with a 'hint' of a fruit juice tends to be artificially sweetened and flavoured. The best advice is to avoid them.

Squashes
Squashes have always been popular because they are cheap and you can

dilute them fairly heavily. They are, however, mainly sugar syrups, and even reduced-sugar brands are high in calories and very bad for dental health. Highly sweetened drinks actually increase the body's need for water, so they are not the best option for quenching thirst.

Fruit squash must by law contain 25% fruit juice for undiluted citrus squash, and 10% for non-citrus fruit squash.

Barley water must contain at least 15% fruit juice when undiluted. It also contains citrus (or other) juice, sugar and barley flour.

Fruit drinks are sold ready-diluted or as concentrates. Concentrates must contain at least 7% whole fruit and 10 to 15% sugar, plus some preservatives. Ready-diluted fruit drinks sold in cartons have no restriction on fruit or sugar content.

High-juice fruit squashes usually contain 35 to 50% fruit juice, but there is no legal limit, so watch the carton.

Most importantly, however, watch out for 'sugar-reduced' brands. These often contain artificial sweeteners, which can be dangerous for health (see page 48).

If you have access to fresh, diluted fruit juice, this is your best option. If you are limited to squash, choose a high-fruit, low-sugar brand, and dilute it heavily.

Fruit and Vegetable Juice

Fresh fruit juice is considered to be the equivalent of a serving of fresh fruit, and will contain at least the recommended daily intake of vitamin C. In fact, fresh fruit and vegetable juices are essential parts of anti-cancer diets. Raw juices do most of the things that solid raw foods do, but in a way that places minimum strain on the digestive system. The concentrated vitamins, minerals, trace elements, enzymes, sugars and proteins they contain are absorbed into the bloodstream almost as soon as they reach the stomach and small intestine.

If you are worried about the number of fresh vegetable and fruit servings you are getting throughout the week, consider purchasing a juicer and making your own fresh juices regularly. Carrot and orange is a particular favourite. Try a glass of carrot and apple juice after a sleepless night and you will experience an astonishing energy boost. Orange and kiwi is good, as is cucumber, apple and lemon. Mix fruits and vegetables together for delicious taste combinations. Fresh fruit juices should be poured on to ice as soon as they are prepared, to reduce oxidation. Sealed, they can be kept in the refrigerator for several hours.

Vegetables Juices

Vegetable	Benefits	Special Notes
Beetroot	Builds up red blood cell count. May help with menstrual problems. The juice from the leaves has oestrogenic or hormonal properties and is used to increase fertility. Cleans the liver, kidney and gall bladder.	Too strong to be drunk on its own. Blend with other juices.
Cabbage	Used for treating stomach ulcers and constipation. Helps to clear gum infection.	Strong tasting; better drunk in a blend with other juices.
Carrot	Aids digestion, tones the hormonal systems, cleanses the skin and may help to prevent cancer. Fights juices. infection and calms the nervous system.	A good base for other fruit and vegetable juices.
Celery	Detoxifies, and used in the treatment of arthritis, diabetes, circulation and heart problems, varicose veins, kidney stones. Helps maintain the balance of fluids in the body, and balances the nervous system.	Good with carrot juice. Juice the tops too.
Cucumber	Natural diuretic, promotes hair growth and regulates blood pressure. May help alleviate rheumatism.	Works quickly, and can be drunk after meals to cleanse.
Parsley	Good for adrenal and thyroid glands, and for maintaining healthy genito-urinary system. Can also treat eye disorders.	Should be taken in small quantities in a blend.
Spinach	Cleanses the digestive system, cures constipation, and works to heal the lining of the entire tract, in particular the colon and small intestine. Can help to speed up digestion.	Best combined, since it can be strong tasting.

Fresh fruit and vegetable juices are high in fibre, and may need to be diluted for children, to avoid runny bowel movements. They are also high in natural sugars, so should not be drunk too much between meals, when sugars can damage your teeth. Diluted juices are always best served with meals.

Next best are freshly squeezed juices available from the supermarket. Remember, however, that they begin to lose their nutritional value from the moment they are opened. You are better off buying small cartons and finishing them within a few hours.

Juices made from concentrates tend to be much higher in sugar and lower in vitamins and minerals. They are, however, much more nutritious than squashes and fizzy drinks, and are best drunk diluted with fresh water. They can also have many of the same therapeutic benefits of fresh fruits and juices. Research shows that apples are excellent detoxifiers, and apple juice - even off the supermarket shelf - can destroy viruses in the body.

Easy Ways to Drink More Water
- Keep a jug of chilled filtered or bottled water within reach in the fridge. If it's the easiest drink to hand, you'll be more likely to drink it.
- For hardened squash drinkers, gradually dilute the amount of syrup until you are drinking mostly water.
- As an alternative to fizzy drinks, buy sparkling mineral water and add your own fruit juices. You can come up with some fun concoctions.
- Consider investing in a water-cooler, which can serve chilled purified water at the touch of a button. You may use it first for its novelty value, but it will undoubtedly become a way of life.
- Buy a plastic bottle and keep it filled in the refrigerator. It will need to be washed and refilled daily to prevent a build-up of bacteria. Take it with you wherever you go.

The Bottom Line

The verdict is pretty clear: water is your best choice, and the healthiest option. Next best are fresh fruit and vegetable juices, and herbal teas in moderation. Alcohol, tea and coffee have the potential to cause health problems, but in moderation are acceptable. All of us have different responses to things like sugar, alcohol and caffeine, and only you will know when you've had too much, or when over consumption is starting to affect your health. Drink wisely, and you'll be amazed at the difference it can make.

Chapter Six

The Supplement Story

Ideally, a healthy diet should include all of the nutrients we need for health. Unfortunately, however, many of us don't eat well enough, and even when we do, much of the food that we eat is nutritionally inferior. We now know that conventionally farmed food often contains fewer nutrients, largely because the soil in which it is farmed is so depleted, it is force-grown, possibly genetically modified, sprayed with pesticides, herbicides and other chemicals, and then left to 'ripen' in the back of a lorry or the cargo hold of an aeroplane. It can be weeks before it reaches our supermarket shelves, by which time what little goodness there might have been has been even further compromised.

Animal products aren't much better. Animals who are fed with feed that does not contain the necessary elements of nutrition, who lead a stressed existence in close confines with other animals, who are pumped full of antibiotics, growth-promoters and other drugs, cannot represent good nutritional value for consumers. And then there's the processing - more than two-thirds of the food that we eat in the Western world has been processed: stripped of its nutrients (although some can be added back in), heat-treated, possibly irradiated, and blended with an astonishing array of additives, colorants, preservatives, fillers and other chemicals.

This is where supplements come in. It's a fairly straightforward concept - replacing missing nutrients with a dietary supplement. First, though, let's clarify the issues:

- Supplements are only effective when they form part of a healthy diet. They're a good idea to make up for areas where your diet isn't perfect, but don't rely on them to correct the effects of an unhealthy lifestyle. They'll do a great deal to help balance problem areas, but they won't undo damage caused, or prevent it from returning in the future.

- A healthy diet can't be manufactured and sold in a bottle. We need fibre, water, protein, carbohydrates and fats for health, and while many components of these can be found in supplemental form, the majority of their health-giving properties cannot.

- Don't believe outrageous claims. If there is a need for a nutrient, your body will make use of it and you will undoubtedly feel better. Some supplements contain substances that work much like drugs, and can alleviate a problem fairly quickly. Others will take much longer, as your health is slowly restored. But remember, they aren't miracle cures.

- When in doubt, see a nutritional therapist who can pinpoint deficiencies and work out a programme that suits your individual needs.
- Most supplements (apart from a good multi-vitamin, EFAs and mineral tablet) only need to be taken for a few months to have effect, and then sporadically after that. No one needs to take the same supplements month after month unless they are aimed at treating a chronic health problem.

Having said this, nutritional deficiencies are becoming increasingly common, given the pollution, junk food and toxins with which we are in regular contact. If you've been able to make changes towards a healthy diet, you will notice a change in the way you are feeling. If you still don't feel as well as you should, there may well be a small deficiency at the root of the problem. And that's when supplements come into their own.

Am I Deficient?

Some obvious and not-so-obvious symptoms rear their heads when there is vitamin or mineral deficiency:

Problem	Possible deficiency
Chronic constipation (not linked to fibre intake)	B-complex vitamins
Chronic diarrhoea (not linked to fibre intake or illness)	Niacin (B3) and vitamin K
Eye problems	Vitamin A
Fatigue	Zinc, iron, vitamins A, B, C, D
Hair problems	Vitamins B12, B2, B6, E and selenium
Recurrent infections	Vitamins A and C, B-complex, calcium, iron, potassium
Muscle cramps	B vitamins, vitamin D
Nervousness or anxiety	B6, B12, B3, magnesium, vitamin C
Skin problems	Vitamins A, B-complex, E, copper, biotin

If you have concerns about deficiency, try a multi-vitamin and -mineral tablet first. Check the label to ensure that the appropriate elements are there. Some tablets contain only a few vitamins. Others contain the whole range. Go for the latter. Give it a couple of weeks - if symptoms don't clear up, consider a trip to a nutritional therapist.

Which Supplements?

On page 41 we discussed the idea of supplementing essential fatty acids in the form of cod liver oil and flaxseed oil. There are other key nutrients which should be considered, according to your individual health, diet, environment and exercise levels:

- A multi-vitamin and - mineral tablet. Look for 'slow-release' tablets if you can find them. Take the tablets according to manufacturers' instructions, and always with food to make sure they are properly assimilated.
- Chewable tablets are fine, but they can damage teeth if they are eaten between meals. Sugar-free is always best or, if you find these unpalatable, look for tablets sweetened with a small amount of fruit sugar.
- For small children, powders and drops are available. Mix them in with food or a little juice. Don't be alarmed by brightly coloured urine - this is normal.

Above and beyond this, consider the following:

- If you suffer from recurrent infections (colds, coughs and ear infections), make sure that you get extra vitamin C. About 1 g (1,000 mg) a day is normally considered to be appropriate, although a nutritional therapist might suggest higher doses.
- Similarly, if you or anyone in the house smokes, extra vitamin C is necessary. Adult smokers lose about 25 mg of vitamin C for every cigarette smoked. Use the same dosage mentioned above. The same goes for people living in areas of high pollution.
- With iron-deficiency anaemia on the increase it may be necessary to supplement iron. Most good vitamin and mineral tablets contain iron, and you should never consider supplementing anything beyond this without the advice of your doctor.
- Stress reduces many nutrients in our bodies - in particular the B vitamins. Don't try supplementing any one at a time, unless recommended by a nutritionist. Once again, a good multi-vitamin and mineral tablet should adequately cover the B vitamins, but if you are under considerable stress, a good B-complex tablet containing about 25 mg of each of the key B vitamins will be sufficient.

Given the number of things that deplete calcium from the bones, including smoking, alcohol and fizzy drinks, to name just a few, you might need to consider supplementing calcium. One good source is the new 'calcium-enhanced' orange juices, which contain a whole day's supply in one glass. Alternatively, talk to your doctor about special supplements, or visit a nutritional therapist.

Antioxidants

Vitamins, minerals and enzymes called antioxidants (including vitamin A, beta-carotene, vitamins C and E and the minerals selenium and zinc) help to protect the body from the formation of 'free radicals'. Free radicals are atoms or groups of atoms that can cause damage to cells, impairing the immune system and leading to various degenerative diseases such as heart disease and cancer. Free-radical damage is believed to be the basis for the ageing process as well.

- Antioxidants have been proven to reduce and in some cases reverse heart disease. Considering the fact that even young children are showing early signs of heart disease, including clogged arteries, making antioxidants part of your diet can make a big difference to your future health.
- One study showed that rates of high blood pressure are approximately two times higher in those with a lower intake of the antioxidant vitamin C in their diet. Vitamin C has a powerful effect on the brain, and is known to reduce the risk of cancer, heart disease, cataracts and other degenerative conditions.
- Vitamin E has been found to enhance a variety of immune system responses, reduce blood stickiness, reduce the harmful effects of toxins such as cigarette smoke, reduce damage caused by the sun (when applied as an oil), halve the risk of heart attack in those with heart disease, prevent cataracts and, with vitamin A, improve some cases of hearing loss. Vitamin E is essential for skin health - age spots are one of the key deficiency signs.
- Selenium decreases the rate of cancer, and increases life span. Selenium deficiency is also signalled by age spots, cataracts, cancerous changes, infections, muscle inflammation and heart disease, so it has an undoubted effect on many parts of the body. Selenium supplements have been found to improve kidney function, help prevent liver cancer, enhance immune function, improve thyroid function, treat skin conditions and reduce the symptoms of arthritis.
- Antioxidants significantly reduce the risk of cancer at virtually all cancer sites - largely by ensuring that carcinogenic chemicals do not attach themselves to our cells.

Other Supplements

Acidophilus

Acidophilus (also known as *lactobacillus acidophilus*) is a source of friendly intestinal bacteria (flora). Healthy bacteria play an important role in our bodies, and unless continually supplied with some form of lactic acid or lactose (such as acidophilus) they can die, causing a host of health problems. Many doctors and health practitioners recommend taking acidophilus alongside oral antibiotics, which can cause diarrhoea, destroy the healthy flora of the intestines and lead to fungal infections. The best source is natural, unflavoured 'live' yoghurt. Acidophilus is not toxic and can be taken daily, with food, in unlimited amounts. Many practitioners recommend taking it as a daily supplement. It is safe for children and is available in chewable, vanilla-flavoured tablets, as well as capsules and powders. Keep it in the refrigerator.

In summary, acidophilus:
- keeps the intestines clean
- prevents yeast infections of the vagina
- aids the absorption of nutrients in food
- can eliminate bad breath (caused by intestinal putrefaction)
- can relieve and prevent constipation and flatulence
- can aid in the treatment of acne and other skin problems
- maintains intestinal health

Bee Propolis
A resinous substance collected from various plants by bees. As a supplement it is an excellent aid against bacterial infections. It is believed to stimulate white blood cells, which destroy bacteria. Studies show that it is good for inflammation of the mucous membranes of the mouth, dry coughs, halitosis, tonsillitis, mouth ulcers and acne, and for boosting immunity.

Essential Fatty Acids
(See page 40).

Fish Oils
A good source of Omega-3 essential fatty acids. Try to go for salmon oil, or Norwegian cod liver oil, which is milder tasting and uncontaminated.

Evening Primrose Oil
This contains the highest amount of gamma-linolenic acid (GLA) of any food substance. This fatty acid is known to help prevent hardening of the arteries, heart disease, MS, high blood pressure, hyperactivity, skin problems, some arthritis (including juvenile) and liver problems.

Garlic
- Reduces the risk of heart disease
- Cleanses the blood and helps to create and maintain healthy bacteria (flora) in the gut
- Helps to bring down fever
- Acts as an antiseptic, with antibiotic and anti-fungal actions.
- Tones the heart and circulatory system
- Boosts the immune system
- Helps to reduce high blood pressure
- Treats infections of the stomach and respiratory system
- Acts as an antioxidant and decongestant.

Garlic is widely used in cooking, but heat destroys its medicinal effects, so it is best to use it only slightly cooked, or raw, or to take it in supplement form.

Amino Acids
These are organic compounds which comprise the 'building blocks' of proteins. A number of amino acids play an essential role in our bodies. Some are classified as essential nutrients - that is, necessary in the human diet - to make almost all elements in the body, including hair, skin, bone, tissues, antibodies, hormones, enzymes and blood. Experts suggest that amino acids should not be supplemented without the supervision of a trained practitioner.

Algae and Other 'Green' Foods
Algae are plants which grow in water. *Spirulina*, one of the most common types, are blue-green bacteria or algae, which are rich in GLA (gamma-linolenic acid) and a wide variety of nutrients, including beta-carotene. Recently there have been a number of cases of algae contamination because some algae is grown outdoors in open lakes. Some symptoms of contamination have included hair loss. Deep-sea algae products are believed to be less likely to be contaminated, and therefore safer.

Seaweeds are another form of 'algae' and are believed to have antiviral activity. Some studies have concluded that they act as a preventative for cancer. Seaweeds are also useful for reducing the damage done by chemo- and radiotherapy. Seaweeds are believed to be natural antacids, and are often used in the treatment of intestinal disorders.

Co-enzyme Q10
CoQ10 is a vitamin-like substance found in all cells of the body. It is biologically important since it forms part of the system across which electrons flow in the cells in the process of energy-production. When it is deficient,

the cells cannot function effectively and the rate at which the muscle cells work is adversely affected. Clinical studies attribute to it the following properties:
- stimulates the immune system and enhances immunity
- improves heart-muscle metabolism
- anti-ageing
- necessary for healthy functioning of the nervous system and the brain cells
- boosts energy levels.
- used in the treatment of gum disease.
- may help in the treatment of obesity

Co-enzyme Q10 is found in organ meats, spinach, polyunsaturated vegetable oils and cold water fish such as tuna and sardines.

Polyphenols and Flavonoids
Polyphenols, which are also known as polyphenolic flavonoids, are powerful antioxidants related to tannins, and found in green tea and red grapes. Flavonoids, also known as bioflavonoids, are colourful antioxidants found in plants (they are responsible for the colours of fruits). There are 12 basic classes of flavonoids, and apart from their antioxidant qualities they are known to help strengthen capillary walls and may be useful in the treatment of heavy menstrual bleeding.
Some flavonoids, such as quercetin, rutin, curcumin and green tea, are anti-inflammatories, helping to form prostaglandins. Best sources include citrus fruits, apricots, cherries, green peppers, broccoli and lemons. The central white core of citrus fruits is the richest source. Bioflavonoids are not toxic, and should be taken with vitamin C for best effect. Studies show that they:
- protect capillaries
- protect against cerebral and other haemorrhaging
- reduce menstrual bleeding
- have antioxidant properties (see page 75), and encourage vitamin C's own antioxidant qualities
- have anti-viral, anti-inflammatory and anti-allergy activity

Super Supplements
Ginseng is sometimes known as 'the root of immortality'. It is both rejuvenating and a tonic, and boosts immune activity and, brain function and reduces the effects of fatigue. Ginseng improves vision and acts to reduce the effects of environmental, physical and emotional stress. More and more of us are using it to balance the strains of busy lifestyles, and it can

have a dramatic effect on energy levels, which tend to decline as we get older.

- Ginkgo biloba is used by the Chinese to promote longevity. Many studies show that it has the ability to alleviate the symptoms associated with ageing, such as poor memory and hearing.
- Gluthatione is an amino acid compound that is a valuable antioxidant and detoxifier. It's a potent free-radical scavenger and mental-booster that also acts as a mood-elevator, and it has the added effect of destroying ammonia, which interferes with brain function.

Children and Supplements

Most children will benefit from a good multi-vitamin and mineral tablet, and there are other nutrients that can make a difference to their overall health and development. It's not a good idea to play around with different supplements unless you are sure that your child needs them or you are working to address a particular health problem. Exceptions to this rule are:
- EFAs (see page 40), which have a body of research behind them. Studies show that these oils can help behaviour, learning and health problems. For example, when these problems were compared between boys with high and low intakes of essential fatty acids, more behavioural problems were found in those with low Omega-3 intakes, and more learning and health problems were found in those with lower Omega-6 intakes.
- Vitamin C, which can help to boost immunity and which acts as an important antioxidant (see page 75).
- Zinc, if your child suffers from recurrent infections, and/or is a faddy eater. Studies show that many faddy eaters have a zinc deficiency. Increase your child's intake of zinc-rich foods, and look for zinc tablets in lozenge form, which can be easily sucked by children.

During Pregnancy

Even the slightest nutritional deficiencies can have serious effects on the health of your growing baby, and the idea that birth defects are often caused by nutritional imbalances in the mother are rapidly gaining acceptance. Slight deficiencies of vitamins B1, B2 and B6, folic acid, zinc, iron, calcium and magnesium have been linked to birth abnormalities. Spina bifida, for example, has been strongly linked to a lack of folic acid in the mother's diet. A survey of 23,000 women found that those who supplemented their diets during the first week of pregnancy had a 75% lower incidence of neural tube defects than those who did not.

It is important, however, not to take too many supplements when you are pregnant. An overabundance of any one nutrient can lead to imbalance. Supplements will never replace a healthy diet, but they can address minor imbalances and deficiencies, and help to ensure that your baby develops well and has every possible chance of a healthy future.

Iron

Iron is an essential ingredient of haemoglobin, which carries oxygen in your blood, and as much as a third of your iron intake is used by your baby to make blood and build up stores for after the birth. Iron deficiency is common in pregnancy and can lead to many uncomfortable symptoms.

Iron-rich foods include: dried fruit, eggs, beef, sardines, brewer's yeast, cocoa, wholegrain bread, beets, broccoli and leafy green vegetables.

Folic Acid

Folic acid is required in twice the normal quantity during pregnancy, to help build red blood cells, and to develop your baby's nervous system.

Good sources include: leafy green vegetables, root vegetables, oysters, mushrooms, almonds, orange juice and dates.

Vitamins B6 and B12

Not only do these vitamins help to ease morning sickness by balancing a hormone called HCG, which is believed to cause the problem, but they are essential for your baby's development. These vitamins ensure the healthy function of the nervous and digestive systems and are essential for energy production. Vitamin B12 in particular is involved in growth and development and the production of red blood cells. It also helps the body to use folic acid.

Good sources include: poultry, fish, eggs, whole grains, nuts, bananas, soya beans and dairy products.

Zinc

The mineral zinc helps to encourage growth and healing, and there is some evidence that it may help to prevent nausea. A 1990 study showed that zinc deficiency in pregnancy is associated with miscarriage, toxaemia, anaemia, abnormally prolonged pregnancy and difficult delivery. In babies it is associated with decreased immunity, learning or memory disorders and birth defects.

Good sources include: beef, seafood, nuts, carrots, corn, bananas and wholegrains.

Magnesium
Magnesium is necessary for calcium metabolism, and it helps promote healthy bones, teeth and muscles, among other things. A Scandinavian study showed that there was a significant reduction in pregnancy-induced high blood pressure when magnesium was supplemented. Babies born to magnesium-treated mothers also spent fewer days in the neonatal intensive care unit.

Good sources include: wholegrain cereals, wheatgerm pulses, nuts, seeds, dried fruits and green vegetables.

Calcium
Calcium is essential for the healthy development of bones and teeth, and is a natural tranquilliser, ensuring the normal function of nerves and muscles.

Good sources include: salmon, broccoli, sesame seeds, soy beans, dairy produce and sprouted seeds.

B-complex vitamins
The B-complex vitamins are crucial for the normal function of the nervous system, and they have a range of other important functions in the body.

Good sources include: yeast, eggs, organ meats, soy beans, fish, wheatgerm, avocados and nuts.

Beta-carotene
Beta-carotene is essential during pregnancy both for its antioxidant activity and to ensure that your baby develops normally.

Good sources include: brightly coloured fruits and vegetables, in particular carrots.

Vitamin C
Vitamin C will help your body to absorb iron, boost your immune system, and establish a good immune system in your baby, which will kick into action when he or she is born. Vitamin C is also a natural antibiotic, and helps your body to fight infection and illness.

Good sources include: leafy green vegetables, citrus fruits, strawberries, blackcurrants, raspberries, watermelon, potatoes and cabbage.

A Sensible Supplement Programme During Pregnancy
● Take a good multi-vitamin and mineral tablet with high levels of antioxidants and zinc. Antioxidant vitamins and minerals help to prevent cell damage caused by oxidation, which can be crucial as your baby is developing.

- Avoid taking more than 10,000 IU of vitamin A, which can cause birth defects in your unborn baby. Take vitamin A as beta-carotene, which is safer.
- Take a zinc supplement (15 mg per day).
- Calcium supplements are also important during pregnancy. Take 500 mg daily, over and above that contained in your multi-vitamin and mineral tablet.
- Take at least 200 mcg of folic acid, which will help to prevent birth defects such as spina bifida.
- B vitamins are crucial to the development of a healthy nervous system and, indeed, a healthy baby! Take 20 mcg of vitamin B12 and 200 mg of vitamin B6 as part of a good B-complex tablet.
- Would-be fathers should take 1,000 mg (1 g) of vitamin C daily in the preconceptual period, as well as 200 IU of vitamin E and extra zinc (up to 25 mg daily), which can increase sperm count, mobility and quality.

There are many, many more supplements that are commonly used for people of all ages, and many herbal products used alongside as well. The best advice is to see a registered practitioner, who will advise you on the best therapeutic supplements for your individual needs.

Chapter Seven

Balancing Your Weight

If you've ever tried unsuccessfully to lose weight, you'll know that diets don't work. Relying on quick-fix solutions doesn't provide us with the desired long-term effect. The fact that diet books and slimming aids sell by the millions, yet more than 50% of Britons are overweight, is fairly clear evidence that something is amiss.

In the UK some 45% of women and 33% of all men consider themselves to be overweight, and a whopping 82% realise that the best way to achieve long-term weight loss is to make small changes to their eating patterns over the course of a year or so rather than go on a radical diet. Nevertheless, more than 70% are on a weight-loss diet at any one time, even though studies show that 95% of all weight loss achieved by this method is usually regained within a year.

Overweight is more than a cosmetic issue. It can have dramatic ramifications on our everyday and long-term health. Heart disease, diabetes, high blood pressure, arthritis, cancer and fatigue are only some of the conditions linked with overweight. There's every reason to lose excess weight before it becomes a problem.

What's the Secret?

The secret to losing weight is not, as countless experts over the past decades have insisted, through calorie-counting diets. Calorie counting requires an attitude of self-denial and an artificial, obsessive approach to food. If you drastically cut down your calorie intake for as few as 48 hours, your body thinks it is being starved, and reacts by slowing down your metabolism. A slower metabolism means that you need less fuel, or food, to maintain your body weight. Starvation diets also lead to bingeing and an unhealthy view of food in general. And it's not fat that your body burns when it thinks it's starving, it's muscle, and we need our muscles to burn calories. Losing weight naturally can be achieved by changing your attitude to food, and making an effort to become fit. When you are fit you are able to burn calories more efficiently, and actually to eat more without putting on weight.

The first step towards successful weight loss is accepting yourself as you are. Weight loss won't change your personality, and it won't make your life dramatically different. What *will* make a difference is taking steps towards good health. Everyone needs motivation to make changes, and feeling good about yourself and having a real desire to do what's best for your health are key to long-term success. When you start seeing the benefits of lifestyle changes, you'll be encouraged to continue.

More importantly, however, it's important to realise that a healthy diet is the one and only way to maintain a healthy weight. Whether you are overweight or underweight, a balanced eating plan will help you to achieve the weight that is right for you. There are several reasons for this:

- A healthy diet prevents swings in blood sugar that can cause cravings for the wrong types of foods.
- You'll be getting all the vitamins and minerals you need for health (with a little supplemental help, perhaps), which means that you won't experience those annoying bouts of fatigue or low energy that lead you to eat … the wrong types of foods.
- You'll feel full and satisfied for longer after meals, because healthy foods tend to be those that confer a sustained release of energy, and their fibre content encourages your digestive system to work effectively and efficiently.
- You'll have a much more balanced view of eating, and you'll find that you are content with the odd treat, rather than being obsessive. After all, there is nothing more tempting than something forbidden. A healthy diet is a plan for life, not a short-term, quick-fix solution, so overeating one day will not send you into a frenzy of bingeing, as it might if you know you've blown your 'diet'.
- Your sense of wellbeing will improve, which means that you will feel better about yourself. It's no secret that people who feel good about themselves are more likely to take care of themselves, and that will encourage you to continue to eat well.

Top Tips for Finding (and Maintaining) Your Natural Weight

- Eat at least seven servings of fresh fruit and vegetables each day. Work your other foods around them, concentrating on quality rather than quantity. When good-quality foods form the basis of your diet, you'll find that you have little room or appetite for fatty foods and those that are nutritionally substandard. Eating whole, fresh foods means you are much more likely to get the nutrients your body needs for balance. Weight loss will not be dramatic, but you can expect to lose about a pound a week just by making this simple change to your diet, and you'll experience improved energy levels and mood, all of which help to sustain the weight loss.

- Eat little and often, which gives your body a chance to digest and process the energy from your food more efficiently. It is better to eat your largest meal at midday, which gives your body time to digest and use it before sleeping. Disrupted sleep is often the result of late-night eating, and you'll find that the energy that should be going into cell repair and rejuvenation is spent on digestion. In the long term this can create imbalances that cause a sluggish metabolism and fat deposits. Furthermore, one recent study indicates that inadequate sleep can actually slow down your metabolism.
- Listen to your body and eat when you are hungry. If you aren't hungry at lunchtime, have a series of small, healthy snacks instead. This will keep your blood sugar stable and ensure that you get the energy you need.
- Enjoy your food. Food is sensual, and you don't need a lot to experience its effects. You'll find that if you eat well, your cravings for sweet and fatty things will diminish, and you are more easily satisfied.
- Forget dieting. Concentrate on enjoying what you eat instead. Dieting creates an obsession with food, and the end result is that it is never far from our thoughts. If you concentrate instead on eating good, healthy fresh food when you are hungry, there is no doubt that weight loss will be achieved.
- Always eat breakfast. It jump-starts the metabolism at the beginning of the day and prevents your body from heading towards starvation mode.
- Consider having yourself tested for food allergies. Many people who have eliminated problem foods from their diets find that their weight quickly stabilises. If you suffer from low energy, abdominal bloating, sleep problems and recurrent headaches, you may have a food-related disorder.
- Drink plenty of water every day. This will help your body flush out toxins and cleanse your digestive system, making it work more effectively.
- Take some exercise. Join a class or find a form of exercise that you can fit into your busy lifestyle. Walking is the newest approved form of exercise. Walking for only 30 minutes per day at a brisk pace burns off more than 2,000 calories a week, with the added benefit of making you fit. Exercise also builds muscle, which is what we need to burn fat.
- Work on improving your self-esteem. Hold yourself properly. Wear clothes that fit. A good attitude may make you feel more energetic, which translates itself into an improved sense of wellbeing. Studies show that when you are feeling well, you are less hungry and tired - which in turn may help you to lose unwanted pounds.

It will come as no surprise that Nature has a trick or two up her sleeve. Many dieters and chronically overweight people have nutritional deficiencies or imbalances that may make it more difficult to shift the necessary kilos. Furthermore, there are many herbs and other supplements that can work to improve your metabolism and mood and even reduce appetite. Good health involves balance, and when you get it right, natural weight loss will follow.

- Chromium may be the dieter's best friend. A mineral responsible for the GTF (glucose tolerance factor) in our bodies, it reduces sugar cravings. Chromium also helps to control levels of fat and cholesterol in the blood. One study showed that people who took chromium picolinate over a 10-week period lost an average of 4.5 pounds (about 2 kg) of fat more than those taking a placebo. Supplemental brewer's yeast, which is naturally high in chromium, may have the same effect.

- HCA (hydroxycitric acid) was originally developed by a drug manufacturer. It is a weak acid, with no apparent toxicity, and it is extracted from the rind of the tamarind fruit (*Garcinia cambogia*). HCA slows down the production of fat and reduces appetite. One study into the fat-burning effects of HCA showed that an average, healthy overweight person could expect to lose in the region of 12 pounds (5 kg) in an 8-week period.

- Acidophilus and other healthy bacteria can help to enhance digestion, which means that nutrients are better absorbed and waste is better eliminated. A sluggish metabolism is often the result of inadequate digestion, and getting it moving can have a positive effect on overweight.

- Co-enzyme Q10 helps the body's cells use oxygen and generate energy. As we get older, we may become deficient in this vitamin-like substance, which results in reduced energy and a general slowing down of body processes. One study showed that people on a low-fat diet doubled their weight loss when supplementing CoQ10 compared with those who did not take it.

- Fibre can help to promote weight loss by filling the stomach and by stimulating the release of hormones that suppress appetite. Fibre also promotes the transport of fats and calories through the digestive system, lowering the amount absorbed by the blood and stored in the body.

- B-complex vitamins have been linked with improved function of the thyroid gland and fat metabolism. Transporting glucose from the blood into the cells depends on the presence of the vitamins B3 (niacin) and B6, and the minerals chromium and zinc. The actual breakdown of glucose into energy depends upon vitamins B1, B2, B3, B5 and C, iron, and co-enzyme Q10. It's essential that all of these nutrients are present in your diet if weight loss is to be successful.

- Vitamin C is also necessary for normal glandular function and can speed up a slow metabolism, prompting it to burn more calories.

- Lecithin (taken as granules or capsules) is a fat emulsifier, breaking down fat so that it can be removed from the body. Take it before meals for best effect.

- Zinc is a key mineral in appetite control. Zinc also functions, together with vitamins A and E, in the manufacture of the thyroid hormone which helps to govern our energy levels and metabolism.

- Calcium is involved in the activation of lipase, an enzyme that breaks down fat for utilisation by the body. Research at Purdue University in Indiana reveals that a high consumption of calcium slows weight gain for women aged 18 to 31 years. These findings confirm that calcium not only helps keep weight in check, but can be associated specifically with decreases in body fat.

- GLA (gamma-linolenic acid) is the active ingredient in borage oil, blackcurrant seed oil, flaxseed oil and evening primrose oil, and it helps to control the metabolism of fats. Taking supplements of GLA helps to control the appetite.

- A good vitamin and mineral supplement is essential. Our diets tend to be notoriously low in nutrients, and any imbalances can cause systemic changes in the body which lead to less energy and a greater disposition towards laying down fat. If you've been regularly dieting over the years, chances are you will be deficient in a number of key nutrients.

It's a change of attitude that will have the most effect if you want to find your natural weight. As you are reading this book you have probably decided to make this change. Decide to make health your top priority and, not only will your weight stabilise, but you'll look and feel better than you ever thought possible.

Part Three
Healthy Eating from the Beginning

Health is my expected heaven.

John Keats

Chapter Eight

Food for All

The key to putting the healthy eating advice in the previous chapters into action is *balance*. None of us wants to enter into a regime that cramps our lifestyle, so it's important that we find ways to get the best possible nutrition in line with our individual needs, budget, tastes and, of course, schedule. Making dramatic changes is not the answer, because you'll soon slip back into old, poor eating habits. For a lifestyle diet to be achievable, it has to be practical and long-lasting.

Balance in Practice

Let's consider the average day. If you manage to eat the required number of fruits and vegetables, have a variety of healthy proteins and some good-quality carbohydrates, all washed down with lots of fresh water, then a bit too much wine will not do any real damage. Nor will a piece of chocolate cake at midnight, nor a bar of chocolate, nor a packet of crisps. You get the picture. You haven't ruined your diet because it isn't a 'diet'. This is an eating plan in which the majority (at least 80%) of the foods and drinks you choose are healthy, and based on the food pyramid (see page 33).

There will always be days and weeks where time is short, there are parties or extra work commitments, or when things just slide out of control. In these situations, try to find a way to balance the negative with the positive. If you have to rely on fast food for a short period, then choose those with the fewest chemicals. Boil up a pot of pasta and chop in some fresh tomatoes and basil, add extra vegetables to a frozen pizza, buy some tubs of fresh fruit, ready prepared, or choose takeaways that are bound to be a bit more healthy, such as a Thai curry with lots of vegetables, a thin-crust vegetarian pizza with feta cheese, or even a chicken kebab in pitta bread.

Don't be alarmed if you have a bad day, or even week. It's the overall balance that counts, not the daily or even weekly load. As adults, too many of us are used to diets that we slip into and out of at random. Eating well is a way of life, not a diet, and it should be adopted permanently. The odd slip-up will not make a difference in the long term if you adopt an overall policy of healthy eating. The more good there is in your general eating plan, the less these slip-ups matter.

Most importantly, however, eating well means changing your approach to food. A healthy attitude is as important as healthy food, and all of us need to want what is best for our minds and bodies, now and in the future. Even if the changes are gradual, they must become an accepted way of eating, and an important part of your life. It is never too late to start taking steps towards optimum health and wellbeing.

Breaking It Down

Many of us believe we are eating well until we stop and look at our diets in detail. The same goes for our children. If they are older they may well be eating at school, or out with friends. Younger children and babies may be fed by a childminder or at a nursery, and we may not be aware of exactly what they are getting.

The best place to start is by analysing what everyone in your family eats and drinks for a week. Write it all down, in as much detail as you can. You might have to rely on their memories to some extent, or on the willingness of a nursery or minder to supply details, but it's important that you come up with as accurate a picture as possible.

Then look at how many of the groups outlined in the food pyramid (see page 35) are covered. If you are short on any main group, you'll know where to make changes. You might be surprised by the results. Encourage all family members to be honest about what they are eating. You need to know the worst possible scenario before you can do anything about it.

Starting at the Beginning

Breastfeeding

Every modern parent is aware of the importance of breastfeeding. Ultimately it's a personal decision whether to breast- or bottle-feed, but it's important to reiterate the reasons why breast is best.

Many women find breastfeeding a rewarding and nurturing experience, which establishes a physical bond between them and their baby, and helps to strengthen an emotional one. There are many advantages to breastfeeding, the first and foremost being nutritional. Breast milk provides the ideal balance of nutrients for your baby, and can help protect him or her from infections to which you are already immune. The composition of breast milk also seems to vary with your baby's needs, whereas the composition of formula stays constant. You can put your baby to your breast as often as he or she seems to want it, and the baby will not gain weight too quickly, as he or she may do if bottle-fed.

Breast milk is designed to provide complete nourishment for a baby for several months after its birth. Before milk is produced the mother's breast produces colostrum, a thick, deep-yellow liquid containing high levels of protein and antibodies. A new-born baby who feeds on colostrum in the first few days of life is better able to resist the bacteria and viruses that cause illness. The mother's milk, which begins to flow a few days after childbirth when her hormones change, is a blue-white colour with a very thin consistency. If the mother eats and drinks healthily, the milk provides the baby with the proper nutritional balance.

- The fat contained in human milk, compared with cow's milk, is more digestible for babies and allows for greater absorption of fat-soluble vitamins into the bloodstream from the baby's intestine.
- Calcium and other important nutrients in human milk are also better utilised by babies.
- Antigens in cow's milk can cause allergic reactions in a newborn baby, whereas such reactions to human milk are very rare.
- Human milk also promotes growth, largely due to the presence of certain hormones and growth factors.
- Breastfed babies have a very low risk of developing meningitis or severe blood infections, and have a 500 to 600% lower risk of getting childhood lymphoma. Breastfed babies also suffer 50% fewer middle ear infections.
- Research also indicates that breastfed babies are less likely to become obese children. A study published in the *British Medical Journal* found that the longer the period babies receive breast milk, the greater the benefits, with those breastfed for a year or longer more than five times less likely to become obese. The study found that 4.5% of bottle-fed babies were obese by the time they reached 5 or 6 years old, but only 2.8% of babies given only breast milk after birth were obese when they reached school age.
- Research has also found that bottle-fed children have far higher blood concentrations of insulin, the chemical that stimulates the laying down of fat cells. Obesity while in childhood is known to be a risk factor for developing cardiovascular disease in later life.
- Other research has shown that breastfeeding for the first 15 weeks protects against diarrhoeal and respiratory diseases, ear and urinary tract infections, and also reduces blood pressure.

Bottle-feeding
Feeding your baby from a bottle may nevertheless be the right choice for you, particularly if the idea of breastfeeding does not appeal or you have a busy lifestyle and will be unable to feed your baby on demand. The infant formulas available today are very nearly equivalent in nourishment to breast milk, and you will be able to bond equally well with your baby, for it

is the care that counts, not the feeding method.

Milk Formulas
Many formulas come as a dried powder in a tin, although some are available in a ready-to-drink form. Everything on the market will be safe, with balanced nutrients and added vitamins, although you may need to choose between brands according to your baby's age and special requirements. Most formulas are based on cow's milk, but there are soya-based formulas available for babies who have difficulty digesting cow's milk, or who have allergies or intolerance. You can also get a goat's milk preparation, although some babies do not like the pronounced taste. If you are unsure which to choose, ask for advice from your health visitor or midwife, who will be able to recommend something suitable. Watch out for baby formulas with GM (genetically modified) ingredients. If possible go for an organic formula, which will hold far less risk in the long term. To avoid the possibility of infection, be scrupulous about cleaning.

Weaning
The best advice on weaning is to wait as long as possible. Until your baby is about a year old, she will get most of her nutrition from her milk. Other foods will add a little variety, and introduce her to new tastes, but they should not be relied upon as a source of a balanced diet. Foods introduced too early can cause digestive problems, and even allergies and intolerance. Six months is a good time to start with a little solid food - some rice cereal, a few fruits and vegetables, for example, but leave it longer if you can, particularly if there are allergies of any nature in your family.

Start gradually, introducing new tastes one at a time. Don't be surprised if your baby isn't interested, and rejects anything that doesn't come with a teat on the end of it. If that's the case with your baby, try a few new tastes, and if he or she still won't have it, wait for a few weeks and then try again. Early foods merely supplement milk feeds, and there is no reason to worry if your baby has nothing but milk for the first six or seven months of life.

Your baby may be ready when he or she shows signs of being interested in food - perhaps beginning to reach out for food on your plate when you are eating. Some mothers decide that their baby needs 'more' when they continue to wake repeatedly at night, but beware! This may be unrelated to hunger. A baby's need to feed in the night - towards the end of the first six months - is more likely to be due to the need for comfort than the need for nutrition or food. You may end up starting your baby earlier than you would like in the hopes that he or she will sleep better when, in fact, solids introduced too early can have quite the opposite effect.

Some babies will thrive on milk for the first 12 months, so don't panic if you have a slow beginner. If you wish to stop breastfeeding you can switch to the bottle long before you need to give solid foods. Similarly, it is not advised that you give solid foods to a baby younger than three months. It is now believed that babies' digestive systems are not mature enough to cope with solids before this time, and they will be more prone to food allergies, rashes, diarrhoea and tummy ache if you do.

First Foods
Your baby's first foods are intended to be tastes rather than nutritional supplements, although it is important to choose foods that are nutritious and which will not put any strain on an immature digestive system. In the beginning you will need to puree everything, making it as sloppy as possible, as your baby will suck it rather than eat it until he or she becomes accustomed to different consistencies.

The best first foods, organic where possible, (pureed):
● apple, pear, peaches, apricots, bananas
● parsnips, swede, green beans, squash, sweet potato, cauliflower, carrots, peas, broccoli
● baby rice

After these first foods you can begin to introduce other cereals, such as wheat, oats and barley, to add some variety. Whichever solids you decide to offer, remember to introduce one new food at a time, for three to four days, to give your baby a chance to grow to like it, before offering another food. It may take some time for a baby to become used to a new taste, and it will also give you an opportunity to pinpoint any adverse reactions to specific foods.

These first tastes are not intended to be meals, merely an introduction to the idea of food, so don't panic if your baby gets very little. Let them enjoy the food, and make a mess if they want to. They will need to learn that food, and mealtimes, are pleasant experiences, and if they feel forced to eat, or pick up tension from you, they will begin to make negative associations with food.

Foods to Avoid
Apart from the specific foods mentioned in the sections on allergies and intolerance, there are foods that should be avoided for other reasons:

Pork and lamb	*Wait until your baby is at least 9 months old, because they are too fatty to digest easily*
Food with any salt	*Can put unnecessary strain on the kidneys*

Spices	Can be very gradually introduced after about six or seven months
Sugary foods or drinks	Can encourage a sweet tooth, and promote tooth decay
Fried foods	Not good for babies. Lightly steam foods when you cook them, and avoid using butter or oil.

Once your child is eating a variety of different foods, as close as possible to what you eat yourselves, they can join in with the family diet.

Older Children and Adults

Obviously it's easier if you have a clean slate with which to work, but even the most reluctant eaters will eventually give in and begin to enjoy eating well.

Breakfast

Let's start at the beginning of the day. Breakfast is important for all of us, but it's even more important for children, and here's why:

- For most children, breakfast is the first meal they'll have had in more than 10 hours, and sometimes even longer. Not only is it necessary to balance out blood sugar levels, but a good breakfast can have a dramatic effect on health and wellbeing. In fact, breakfast is the meal most directly connected to school achievement. Here's what the experts are saying:

- Children do better in the morning hours following a good nutritious breakfast. Their speed, response time and problem-solving skills are improved and they are better able to persevere throughout the morning. Children who skip breakfast have shorter attention spans, do poorly in tasks requiring concentration, and even score lower on standard achievement tests.

- When researchers compared the diets of children who regularly eat breakfast with those who don't, they found that the breakfast skippers never made up for lost nutrients. Children who ate a morning meal took in far more nutrients over the course of the day.

- US researchers from Harvard Medical/Massachusetts General Hospital in Boston recently verified that hungry children are more likely to have behavioural as well as academic problems than children who are properly nourished.

- In a US programme which studied the effects of a breakfast pilot program in six schools, students demonstrated a general increase in maths grades and reading scores, increased attention, fewer nurse visits and improved behaviour.

Not a Natural Breakfast Eater?
Some of us are simply not hungry in the morning, which can make it difficult to ensure we get a balanced breakfast. Children in particular are often
grumpy in the morning (due to low blood sugar, in fact) and may be pickier
than usual. Early morning tears and tantrums over food are, paradoxically,
normally the result of hunger. Don't be tempted to wage a war over the
breakfast table. Once they are dressed and feeling a little more alert, most
children are hungry enough for some breakfast.

● Ask your child to choose breakfast the night before, and have it set up at
  the table when they come down. Some children may feign amnesia,
  but most will be delighted to see a requested item.
● Breakfast doesn't have to mean traditional breakfast foods. There's no
  reason why a slice of healthy pizza, a bowl of soup or a sandwich can't
  be offered instead. The most important thing is to focus on getting a
  good source of unrefined carbohydrates into the meal, to ensure that
  blood sugar levels stay stable throughout the morning, and to get
  some protein, vitamins and minerals, and fats.
● If your child won't eat before school, then make a packed breakfast.
  Add a bit of cheese, an apple, a wholemeal roll and a yoghurt. Juice in
  a box will balance it out. Alternatively, a hard-boiled egg with an
  orange and a wholemeal bun is a good balanced breakfast. An individual box of a healthy cereal can be placed in a bag and eaten without
  milk. Or try one of the milk-and-cereal boxes available - choosing the
  ones with the lowest sugar, salt and additive content.

Breakfast on the Run
No time for more than a cup of coffee in the morning? Consider some of
the following options:

● A boiled egg sliced into a pitta pocket, alongside a peach and a bottle of
  juice.
● A yoghurt, some fresh fruit and an oatcake can be eaten at your desk
  once you get to work.
● Ham, tomatoes and salad in a wholemeal wrap makes for a healthy
  meal to eat on the run.
● A wholemeal muffin, with raisins or fruit, or yoghurt with dried apricots
  and a wholemeal bun, or a wholemeal teacake with soft cheese and
  fruit spread.
● Whatever you do, avoid breakfast bars, which are unbelievably high in
  sugar.

Lunch
With more and more children eating their lunch at school, many parents

find it worrying that they have so little control over their child's diet during the day. Don't despair. Studies show that children, regardless of income, generally have higher intakes of key nutrients when they eat school lunch.

If your children eat at school, make sure they are aware of the basics of nutrition. Explain how a healthy meal will give them lots of energy for sports or tests in the afternoon, and how it will make them feel happier. Negotiate an eating plan - chips only once a week, for example, ham only once a week, at least two vegetables and one fruit (different every day, if possible) a day. If they know the parameters, and know that they can make the choices based on your agreement, they'll be more likely to stick to a healthy diet. Let them feel empowered rather than ruled. Show an interest in what they've eaten. Most children love reciting what they've had for lunch, right down to the last soggy Brussels sprout. Work out where the strengths and weaknesses are, and base the rest of their daily diet on those. For example, if they've been short on fresh fruits and vegetables at lunchtime, serve a picnic tea with lots of fresh vegetables and dips, a platter of fresh fruit, yoghurt, cheese and wholemeal toast. Even a bowl of fresh vegetable soup can make up for a less nutritious lunch.

Packed Lunches for the Whole Family
Lunchboxes give you a little more control over what your children are eating, although it's difficult to know what has been eaten if the lunchbox comes back empty every day. Children may simply tip out the contents rather than face an irate parent. The main solution is to discuss lunch in advance. Work out what your children want and will eat, and try to incorporate that to some extent. Give a list to choose from; for example, egg salad, cheese and cucumber, tuna and sweetcorn, tomato and salad or peanut butter and banana. Children are also much more likely to eat something upon which they have decided.

The premise for healthy lunches is the same as for other meals. You want balance, nutrition, and as many elements of the food pyramid as possible. Here are some ideas:

FOR CHILDREN
- Fruit doesn't have to be fresh and raw to be nutritious. Little pots of tinned fruits in juice are also healthy and much more appealing to children, and those with no time to prepare anything themselves.
- Peel oranges and tangerines before serving to make the job easier. You can also cut up fruit, but dip it in a little lemon juice before wrapping to prevent discoloration.
- Cut sandwiches into small bite-sized pieces that your child can pick up and eat while chatting to schoolmates.

- Picnic-style lunches are always popular. Choose from a range of: small pieces of cooked chicken, yoghurt, yoghurt-based dips, fruit (such as grapes or strawberries), cheese, wholemeal pitta bread, hummus, boiled eggs, raisins, dried fruits, raw vegetables (such as carrots, broccoli florets, olives, sliced cucumber, sliced peppers, celery and even a small pot of sweetcorn), rice crackers or cheese straws.
- Some children prefer to make their own sandwiches - either at home before school, or at school, if you have supplied the ingredients.
- Hot lunches - for example, leftover soups, stews or pastas - can be kept hot in a vacuum flask. With a piece of fruit and a wholemeal roll, they'll have a completely balanced meal.

Make sure that you keep lunchboxes and flasks clean and dry between use. If you make your lunches in advance, keep the lunchbox (or its contents) in the fridge until your child sets off for school. Better still, invest in an insulated lunchbox with cooling blocks to keep food fresh.

FOR ADULTS
- Tuna fish and salad on a wholemeal bun. If you don't want the sandwich to get soggy, pack the tuna salad separately, and spread it on the bun when you get to work.
- Bagel with cheese and salad. Bagels don't tend to become as mushy as bread, so they are a good option and naturally low in fat. Choose those with seeds, if you can.
- Avocado, tomato and mozzarella with fresh basil and a dash of balsamic vinegar can be added to a normal green salad for a delicious, nutritious meal. Or use as a topping for bagels.
- Pitta bread filled with cooked prawns, lemon juice, a squirt of coconut milk and some water chestnuts and salad.
- Lean roast beef or ham and salad on a wholemeal bun, wrap or bagel.
- Leftover rice makes a healthy salad, with chopped, cooked and raw vegetables, prawns, ham or feta cheese, olives, onions and a light dressing.
- Salad nicoise (tuna, spring onions, olives, chopped cucumbers and tomatoes), lightly cooked green beans and a wholemeal bun.
- Pasta salad with grilled chicken, roasted vegetables, sundried tomatoes, feta cheese and as many cooked and raw chopped vegetables as you can find. Add chickpeas or kidney beans for extra protein and nutrition.
- Chilled vegetable soup, which can be heated up or drunk cool. Again, accompany with a wholemeal bun or piece of toast, a chunk of cheese or a yoghurt, and a piece of fruit.

Super Snacks

Few people can get through the day without a snack or two, and most school-aged children are encouraged to bring one to school for break time. Snacks are important and should never be dismissed as 'fillers' or inconsequential to your overall healthy eating plan. Nor should they be considered 'treats' which fall outside your normal nutritional guidelines. Some of us have little opportunity to eat regular, healthy meals, and snacks are a great way to balance a less healthy diet. In fact, there is nothing wrong with having five or six large 'snacks' instead of three square meals in a day. As long as they are made up of all the nutrients you need on a daily basis, it's a perfectly good way to eat (and easier on the blood sugar).

Snack Ideas
- Fresh fruit
- Dried, unsulphured fruit
- Nuts (after the age of 5, and if there are no allergies). Try a handful of pistachios, which take some time to shell! Seeds, such as sunflower, are also nutritious and easy to eat.
- Toast with peanut butter, yeast extract (but watch the salt content), cheese or a mashed banana
- Fresh popcorn without salt or sugar
- Breadsticks (choose those with seeds, if possible)
- Brown rice cakes (spread them with any of the toast-topping suggestions, or eat plain)
- Yoghurt
- Good-quality biscuits, preferably home-made
- Breakfast cereal with organic milk
- Hummus and pitta bread
- Raw vegetables (cauliflower and broccoli florets, peppers, celery, carrots, cucumbers, mangetout, for example)
- 'Milkshakes' with fresh milk (better still, rice milk), a banana, some fresh fruit juice and a little yoghurt. Freeze a couple of bananas to add to the blender to make the milkshakes creamy cold! Banana skins will turn black and the consistency will be grainy but they provide bulk, flavour and texture to a healthy milkshake.
- Home-made or good-quality cakes, such as carrot or banana
- Raisins
- Cheese
- Pitta bread filled with tasty chicken morsels, tzatziki, grated carrots and chopped cucumber
- Homemade pizza with feta cheese, mozzarella and fresh chopped

vegetables. Cook, then eat hot or cold.

- Wholegrain cereals (with a low sugar content)
- Low-salt pretzels
- A bowl of fresh fruit with Greek yoghurt, Greek honey and some dried fruits
- Chopped fresh carrots, fresh cucumber, sugar-snap peas, mangetout and dwarf sweetcorn with hummus or tzatziki.
- Fresh tuna pate and toasted pitta bread
- Fresh vegetable 'chips': Heat a little olive oil in a baking tray. Cut sweet potato, potato, carrot, parsnip and swede into 'chip-shaped' pieces, toss in the hot oil, and roast at a high temperature until golden brown. Season with black pepper and a little sea salt and serve.
- Fresh fruit salsa with apple juice, chopped kiwi, strawberries, lemon juice, pears, apples, mangoes - in fact anything in season. Brush wholemeal enchiladas with a little organic brown sugar in water, sprinkle with cinnamon and cut into 'nachos'. Bake until crisp and dip in your salsa.
- Fresh tomato salsa with toasted pitta and a little feta cheese
- If you simply can't get through the day without a bag of crisps, choose low-salt brands, and preferably those that are hand-cut and cooked, or made using a variety of different vegetables.

The Dinner Hour

For most people, dinner is the main meal of the day, but it doesn't need to be. In fact, eating your healthy main meal at lunchtime is easier on the digestion (giving your body plenty of time to deal with food before bedtime), will help you to stay alert throughout the day by keeping blood sugar levels stable, and also gives you a much-needed break in what may otherwise be a stressful, busy day. Whenever you choose to eat your main meal (and all of these suggestions are suitable for big lunches, instead), focus on adding as many fruits and vegetables as you can. Your biggest meal should aim to be your most nutritious, so keep an eye on the pyramid, and create an extravaganza.

Healthy Main Meals
- Grilled fish or chicken (marinated overnight if you have time) served with salad, brown rice, courgettes, carrots and green beans
- Vegetarian lasagne (this is easy and quick to make in advance). Use cottage cheese instead of a béchamel sauce, and top with mozzarella cheese. Include loads of roasted or stir-fried vegetables, such as peppers, courgettes, aubergine, onions, spinach, fennel and tomatoes, in a pre-pur-

chased fresh tomato sauce, in the place of your normal meat sauce. Serve with a salad

- Roasted chicken served with potatoes, broad beans, leeks, carrots and cucumber salad
- Grilled fish with lemon, new potatoes, French beans, sweetcorn and salad
- Stew, with lean meat, vegetable stock, potatoes, peas, carrots, swede, celery and onions in a broth. Lightly brown the meat first, to seal in juices and flavour. If you have a slow-cooker, let it simmer throughout the day, and add vegetables that need a shorter cooking time, such as courgettes, peas, sweetcorn or beans, when you arrive home from work.
- Chicken and vegetable kebab, served with rice and salad.
- Chicken curry, dhal, cucumber raita and brown chapatti.
- Stir-fries, with chicken, lean pork, lean sliced beef or fish, can be accompanied by a variety of different vegetables and/or fruits. Season with plenty of fresh herbs, and serve with rice or a baked potato.
- Stir-fry chicken until it is lightly browned, and create your own 'pitta bar', offering chopped cucumber, carrots, salad, tomatoes, cool sweetcorn, celery and even roasted vegetables alongside some tzatziki (Greek yoghurt with mint and cucumber) and warm pitta bread.
- Stir in as many tinned or frozen vegetables as you can muster up into a good bottled tomato sauce and serve with pasta. Top with a little cheese, sunflower seeds and even diced ham, for protein. Serve with a salad.
- Roast pork (with all visible fat removed), fresh apple sauce, potatoes, red cabbage, broccoli and yellow beans

Dessert Ideas
There's nothing wrong with a sweet ending to a meal, and there are many healthy dessert ideas that will appeal to even the most hardened sugar addict! Try some of the following:
- A square of good-quality dark chocolate, melted over a banana and served with yoghurt
- Baked apples with raisins, a little maple syrup, and some yoghurt
- Frozen yoghurt (you can normally freeze fromage frais, or buy a good-quality pre-frozen brand) with walnuts, fresh fruit and maple syrup
- Fresh or frozen strawberries crushed with a little lemon juice and a pinch of cinnamon. Use as a sauce on other fresh (or dried) fruits or plain yoghurt.
- Fruit crumble, heavily doused with cinnamon (which reduces the need for a lot of sugar), a little brown sugar or maple syrup, and raisins (which add natural sweetness). Blend rolled oats with a little more cinnamon, a drop or two of vanilla extract, a teaspoon of sugar, and a pat of butter

as a topping. It's healthy, low-fat and very nutritious.

- Summer pudding, using a light wholemeal bread, and served with yoghurt
- Baked banana cooked in rum and maple syrup, served with yoghurt
- Strawberries, cherries and other summer fruits, soaked in orange juice (with or without a little orange-flavoured liqueur) and poured over yoghurt or a good-quality ice cream

Getting the Most from Your Food

Is Fresh Best?
Fresh foods are almost always best. I qualify that because they are, in some cases, nutritionally inferior to their frozen counterparts. If you buy your foods from a supermarket, make extra certain that they are fresh and ripe and look for the organic section. Many foods have travelled long distances from other countries, or sat in the back of a lorry for long periods of time. Fresh foods, such as fruits and vegetables, become less nutritious the longer they are away from picking. If your fruits or vegetables are unripe, let them ripen naturally in the sun on your kitchen windowsill. This will help to promote nutrient content and improve flavour.

A local greengrocer or health food shop may be a better bet for fruit and vegetable supplies, and all the better if you can find one that sells organic. Supplies are usually fresh as the turnover is high, and the produce collected the same day from the farmers' markets. An organic food delivery service is another good bet, and it can be enormously convenient for busy parents.

Frozen is next best, mainly because it is normally frozen immediately after picking, which preserves the nutrient content. On the whole, frozen foods retain their nutrient content for far longer than fresh foods, so unless you are planning to eat your food within a day or so of buying it, frozen might be best. Some of the textures of fruits and vegetables are altered by freezing, so don't expect the crunch of fresh. They are a great addition to stews, pastas and sauces, however, and are fine eaten on their own if you don't mind a slightly soggier texture.

Tinned fruits and vegetables are less nutritious, and many of the nutrients have soaked into the water, juice or syrup in which they are suspended. Look for brands packed in water and natural juices, and make sure to drink the juice as well. Tinned fish, such as salmon and tuna, may have also lost some of its key nutrients (in particular, essential fatty acids, which may be lost in the canning process), but they are still nutritious provided they are tinned in water, not brine or oil.

Eat the skins of organic fruits and vegetables whenever possible. Many key nutrients are concentrated in the skins. All fruits and vegetables should be washed carefully before eating the skins, although some experts recommend that you peel them before eating. With oranges and other citrus fruits, although these peels are not eaten, the toxins can be absorbed in the oils of the flesh and you can transfer them on to the peeled fruit. Wash the fruit, wash your hands, and then peel it.

Don't cut, wash or soak fruits and vegetables until you are ready to eat them. Exposing their cut surfaces to the air reduces many nutrients. This may mean that advance preparation may be impossible, but your diet will benefit from the freshness of the food.

Which Cooking Method?

Raw fruits and vegetables contain more nutrients (and, it appears, different types of nutrients) than cooked. Raw foods contain enzymes that are required by the body to break down other foods. These enzymes are crucial to the digestive process and without them we are unable to absorb what we need from food, or to process it correctly. More than half the nutrients of foods are destroyed in the cooking process - possibly more, depending on how you cook them. Boiling, for example, causes the majority of nutrients to leach into the cooking water. This is why it is suggested that cooking water be used for stocks, sauces or gravies. Just five minutes of boiling reduces the thiamine content of peas by up to 40%. Similarly, boiling cabbage reduces its vitamin C content by up to 75%. Although vegetables are a good source of vitamin C, we often end up pouring most of it down the sink with the cooking water.

Deep frying oxidises fat and turns essential fatty acids into trans-fats (see page 12). It also adds unnecessary fat to foods, and destroys almost all the nutrients. If you must fry foods, stir-fry using only a little olive oil, and never heat it to smoking point.

Microwaves are acceptable for cooking water-based foods such as vegetables, but not for anything that contains oils, such as fish, nuts or seeds. The majority of essential fatty acids are destroyed in the process, making them far less nutritious.

Steaming is the best way to ensure that the nutrient content is maintained. Use as little water as possible, and steam until vegetables become brightly coloured. It always takes less time than you think.

But there is another side to the coin. A Europe-wide study has shown that the body can absorb more of an important substance from cooked vegetables than from raw ones. This research suggests that cooking can improve the performance of carrots, broccoli and spinach when it comes to protecting health.

So get a balance of both raw and cooked fruits and vegetables in your diet.

Healthy Eating on a Budget

Obviously an entirely organic diet will be more expensive than regular produce, but you can tailor your diet to your budget. Buy organic whenever possible and avoid processed, refined and ready-prepared meals. These foods are actually more expensive in the long run. Compare the cost of a frozen pizza to a home-made one. Using a tin of tomatoes, a handful of herbs, some good-quality cheese and some fresh and frozen vegetables on a good Italian base, you'll still spend less than you would on the average shop-bought variety.

Consider these options:

- Work your eating plan around what's on special offer. If fresh salmon fillets are on sale, buy several and freeze some. Do the same with good-quality meats, freshly squeezed juices, organic milk, organic bread and anything that represents a saving. As long as you eat the food within a few weeks, you'll be getting good nutrition at considerable savings.
- Do invest in a freezer, and use it for leftovers, extra servings of sauces, stews, casseroles and even pasta dishes. Frozen vegetables are often less expensive than fresh.
- Make your own marinades (honey, garlic and lemon juice is an easy base, and you can add whatever herbs you like to it) and use them for meats and vegetable proteins or tofu.
- Meat and fish tend to be the most expensive items on the menu, but it's important to remember that a little goes a long way nutritionally. Buy a good-quality salmon fillet or tuna steak on sale, and a handful of prawns and you have the makings of an delicious and nutritious fish pie.
- Load up on vegetables and pulses, which represent good value for money. Not only are they filling, but they'll provide a wide variety of vitamins, minerals and protein.
- Take the time to cook and bake. Although that may sound unrealistic if you've a busy schedule, it only takes about 5 minutes to mix together a banana cake, for instance. Biscuits can take slightly longer, as they bake in batches, but ask your children to help. Home-made goods are better for the whole family, they can be frozen, they taste better and, once again, they are much cheaper than shop-bought varieties.
- Eat seasonal produce. Some experts believe it is much healthier to eat local foods, and when fruits and vegetables are in season they are much less expensive than varieties flown in from other countries.

As we age our body's requirements change, and it often becomes less efficient at assimilating the nutrients in our food. Worse still, the degenerative effects of ageing often take their toll, with a host of chronic and acute health conditions becoming part of daily life.

The good news is that studies have shown that degeneration - of the mind and body - can be slowed down a great deal by using supplements (prudently) and eating well.

Diet is important at any age, but it's even more so in older age, when we tend to want to eat less. It's obviously hard to fit in all the required nutrients when you simply aren't feeling very hungry, but it's essential to try. Even a mouthful of French beans or a few grapes, for example, will count as a serving of fruits and vegetables if your meals are small and your intake minimal.

Elderly people who are chronically ill are most likely to be at risk of nutritional deficiency. Pain, disability, medications or even badly fitting dentures can make getting and eating an adequate diet very difficult.

What to Do

- Don't be tempted to give up and live on mushy peas and soup. Chop or have someone help you chop or puree vegetables and protein into manageable portions. Freeze them in small containers, for easy access.
- Make nutritious stews, soups and soft pasta dishes. Any of the meal ideas on pages 95 and 101 can be adapted to suit your appetite, taste and requirements.
- Lean muscle tissue is reduced when we age, which makes protein all the more important. Try to get a variety of sources, including pulses, lean meats, cheeses, wholemeal breads, pasta and beans.
- Fibre is increasingly important as we get older. Constipation can be a problem as the digestive system becomes less efficient, particularly if there is inadequate exercise. Laxatives are often used to treat constipation, which rob the body of vital nutrients as they are not properly absorbed. Rather than using bran or laxatives it is best to consume a diet that is high in fibre (see page 17). If wholemeal cereal is not enough, try plenty of fresh fruit juices and increase your intake of water.
- Fruits and vegetables, particularly raw, can be difficult to manage, but they can be cut into small pieces and chewed carefully, which stimulates the saliva and helps to break down the food. Fresh fruits and vegetables are an important source of antioxidants, which will help to discourage the degenerative effects of ageing, and are now known to prevent or halt the course of some cancers. More than ever it is important to include fresh salads, fruits, vegetables and wholegrains in the

daily diet. If it is impossible to eat foods raw, then lightly steam or stew them and mix them with something soft like cous cous (for vegetables) or oatmeal (for fruit).

- Vitamin C is required in increasing amounts in later years, as our immune system becomes more vulnerable to infection. Chronic ill-health or injury also increases the daily requirements for this vitamin. If it is difficult to eat fresh foods, several glasses of fruit or vegetable juice will help to keep levels up. Kiwi fruits, which are easy to eat and fairly soft, are very high in vitamin C, and certainly as affordable as oranges. Other good sources of vitamin C include organic strawberries, broccoli, cauliflower, raspberries and blackberries.
- Vitamin D is needed to transport calcium from the blood to the bones and back again. As the majority of our vitamin D comes from sunlight, the housebound should try to sit in the summer sun whenever possible (with a suitable sunscreen). Alternatively, you may wish to consider a vitamin D supplement.
- Take a good multi-vitamin and mineral supplement, with extra antioxidants (vitamins A, C, E and selenium) to help slow down the ageing process. Antioxidants can help to prevent arthritis, cancer, dementia, heart disease, and adult-onset diabetes, as well as extending life expectancy.
- Ensure that you get plenty of EFAs in your diet (see page 39), choosing foods such as salmon, herring, mackerel, and nuts and seeds, as well as taking an EFA supplement.
- Cut down on fats, and use olive oil, which is the healthiest oil and is associated with longevity and reduced cholesterol and heart disease.
- Ensure that your teeth are cared for and that you have well-fitting dentures if your teeth are not your own. Studies show that poor chewing is a cause of malnutrition in some elderly people. Chewing food produces saliva, which helps to keep your mouth healthy and stimulates the taste buds. If you can't taste your food, you are much less likely to find it interesting.
- Make sure you have company. Loneliness and depression in old age can lead to self-neglect. Try to find time to eat with a friend, or take a sandwich to the local park.

Healthy Eating for Those with Health Problems

Thyroid Problems
Under- and overactive thyroid glands can cause a number of unpleasant symptoms, but a healthy diet can go a long way towards easing the problem. Consider the following:

- Some foods are termed 'goitrogens', which means that they have the ability to block the uptake of iodine from the blood. Iodine is essential for thyroid function, and a deficiency can be the cause of an underactive thyroid condition. Therefore, any food that is a goitrogen will make an underactive thyroid problem worse. Soya is one of these foods, but so are turnips, cabbage, peanuts, pine nuts, Brussels sprouts, broccoli, kale and millet. If you are diagnosed with a severe underactive thyroid problem, you will normally be told to restrict your intake of these foods. When eaten raw, and in excess, problems can occur.
- On the other hand, include reasonable amounts of foods such as seaweed (kelp) which are low in calories and have a very good mineral content including the trace minerals zinc, manganese, chromium, selenium and cobalt, and the macro minerals calcium, magnesium, iron and also iodine.
- Selenium (see page 32) is a very useful mineral for the treatment of an underactive thyroid as it helps to ensure the proper functioning of the thyroid hormones. Low levels of selenium have been linked to underactive thyroid problems.
- Add extra wheatgerm or oatgerm to cereals.
- Avoid all refined foods, food additives, sugar, fatty meats, and alcohol.
- Eat sprouted seeds and beans regularly.
- Eat vegetable protein such as tofu, and pulses, as well as fish, seafood and poultry.
- Ensure all carbohydrate is unrefined and of a wide range of types, mostly coming from vegetables, pulses and soya.
- Increase intake of freshly ground mixed seeds, especially linseeds and pumpkin seeds.
- Increase intake of vegetables, especially watercress, radishes, garlic, and seaweed, and fruit, including dried yellow fruit such as apricots.
- Reduce intake of meat and full-fat dairy foods.
- Use cold-pressed virgin seed oils and olive oil on salads.

Heart Disease
- Cut down on saturated fats, choosing monounsaturates in their place, or good-quality polyunsaturates (see page 40).
- Eat as many vegetables as possible, for their nutrient value.
- Make sure your diet is well balanced and contains plenty of fibre. Eat lots of raw foods. For protein, eat grilled fish and skinless turkey and chicken, which are low in saturated fat.
- Include garlic, onions and lecithin in your diet. These reduce blood cholesterol levels.
- Add raw nuts (except peanuts), olive oil, salmon, trout, herring and

mackerel to your diet, for their EFA content, and take an EFA supplement.
- Avoid stimulants such as coffee and black tea, which contain caffeine. Avoid fried foods, red meats, sugar, chocolate, processed foods, soft drinks, spicy foods and refined flours.
- Eliminate salt from your diet.
- Consider taking a good antioxidant (see page 75).

Arthritis
- Eat mainly a vegetarian diet with a little oily fish two or three times a week.
- Increase intake of antioxidant vegetables and fruit, and bioflavonoids.
- Increase intake of raw and lightly cooked vegetables.
- Drink vegetable juices such as carrot and celery, or watercress, celery and parsley, instead of fruit juice.
- Increase intake of freshly ground mixed seeds, including linseeds.
- Reduce intake of potatoes, tomatoes, bell peppers and eggplants.
- Avoid red meat, dairy foods, saturated fat, salty or pickled foods, food additives, acid fruits (such as berries and citrus fruits), fried foods, tea, coffee, sugar, soft drinks and spirits.
- Consider adding glucosamine to your diet, a vitamin-like substance which has been proved to have a dramatic effect on arthritis symptoms.

Boosting Immunity
Your diet will have an impact on your body's ability to fight off invaders. There are many herbs and other supplements on the market to encourage strong immunity, but your starting point must always be a good, healthy diet. Consider the following:
- Eat a balanced diet rich in whole foods, nuts and seeds, fresh vegetables and fruits, high in fibre, low in saturated fat, and avoid smoking, environmental pollutants, alcohol, fats, refined grains, sweeteners and alcohol, all of which compromise immune activity.
- Take a good multi-vitamin and -mineral supplement to ensure that you have adequate quantities of nutrients with immune-boosting activity. These include vitamin A, B-complex, C, E, and the minerals zinc and selenium.

Foods, herbs and dietary nutrients that are known to boost immunity include:

Garlic   *Helps to prevent infections of all kinds, including those which have become immune to antibiotics. Also helps to cleanse the blood.*

Echinacea	Widely used to treat chronic and acute infections by cleansing the blood and lymphatic system, which stimulates the production of white blood cells and antibodies. Take three weeks on, one week off.
Ginseng	Encourages the body to deal efficiently with stress, as well as stimulating white blood cell production and aiding recovery after illness.
Vitamin A and beta-carotene	Increase both the number and the activity of antibodies such as T-helper cells. Also help the thymus gland to grow, protecting it from the harmful effects of stress. Vitamin A protects the respiratory system from viral infections, and beta-carotene is antioxidant with a good immune-enhancing effect.
Vitamin B6	Can help to keep your immune system working at optimum level, and may help to prevent cancer and the growth of tumours.
Vitamin C	Helps the body resist infection, and works to aid the thymus gland and white blood cells. Studies have shown that viruses simply cannot survive in tissues that have been saturated with vitamin C, so it's worth considering keeping your intake to a high level during cold and flu season, or when you are run down.
Vitamin E	An immune-stimulant that can encourage the body to resist a number of diseases, including some cancers and autoimmune conditions. Also improves antibody response.
Zinc	Necessary for the immune system to function properly, and can prevent a number of viruses from spreading.
Selenium	Antioxidant, can protect the integrity of the cells, improving their overall function.

PMS

Do you suffer from PMS? Chances are that your symptoms are exacerbated or even caused by your diet. Consider the following:

● Many of the symptoms that we associate with PMS are, in fact, the result of blood sugar problems. Follow the advice on page 47.

● Eliminate or drastically reduce your alcohol intake. First, it's important to give your liver a rest so that it can detoxify and excrete old hormones efficiently. Secondly, however, alcohol can cause blood sugar fluctuations.

- If breast tenderness is your main pre-menstrual symptom, you should avoid any drinks or foods that contain caffeine. The active ingredients in caffeine are called methylxanthines, and they have been proven to increase problems with painful, lumpy and tender breasts.
- Magnesium is an important mineral in relation to PMS. It is classed as 'nature's tranquilliser' and is, therefore, vital in symptoms that relate to anxiety, tension, or other emotional states. Choose foods that are high in magnesium (see page 30), and consider supplementing.
- A number of studies have shown that evening primrose oil (EPO) is effective in reducing the symptoms of PMS, and many of the other forms of EFAs (see page 40) will help to balance hormones.

Menopause Symptoms
- Stabilise blood sugar levels by reducing the amount of sugar and refined foods you eat, and make sure that you get complex carbohydrates on a 'little and often' basis. This prevents your adrenal glands from working overtime, which is important because they should be producing oestrogen as your ovaries produce less.
- Avoid tea and coffee, which contribute to the blood sugar problem and also deprive the body of vital nutrients and trace elements.
- Reduce your intake of dairy products and red meat, as these are animal proteins and can increase the amount of calcium you excrete (a risk factor for osteoporosis).
- Ensure your diet contains sufficient essential fatty acids such as oily fish, nuts and seeds. They help to lubricate the joints, skin and vagina as well as performing other functions, such as keeping cholesterol in check and ensuring a healthy metabolism.
- Make sure you are getting enough fibre from good sources (not bran; see page 17). Eat plenty of fresh fruits and vegetables (cooked and raw) and whole grains such as brown rice, wholemeal bread, wholemeal pasta and oatmeal. Fibre helps to keep your blood sugar stable and it encourages the elimination of toxic waste products.

Fitting It All In

It can be difficult to contemplate finding time to shop for and prepare good healthy foods if you have a busy lifestyle, but there are many ways to help make it work:
- Plan menus well in advance, and arrange (by fax or via the Internet) for your groceries to be delivered either from a local supermarket or through one of the good organic box services.
- Make time to pick up fresh foods daily, just as they do in Europe.

- Prepare meals in advance and freeze them for use when the going is tougher.
- Choose a selection of healthy, pre-prepared foods from your local supermarket. A plain cheese pizza can become a vegetable feast with a few additions, or a vegetable lasagne or a fish pie, accompanied by a crisp salad, makes a perfectly good meal if you are in a hurry.
- Consider having lots of small snacks rather than big meals that need a lot of preparation time (see page 98). Try, however, to sit down while you eat (preferably with your family at least once a day), and to enjoy your food. Eating on the run isn't good for digestion or for health.
- Learn some easy ways of cooking, such as slow-cooking and stir-fries, and make use of microwaves and steamers. Grilling a chicken breast takes less time than heating up a pre-packaged meal, so don't be tempted to opt out if you don't have to.
- Make big quantities of rice and pasta in advance, and use them throughout the week with different accompaniments. Both can be frozen, to keep them fresh, rice keeps well in the fridge for about 3 or 4 days.
- Consider cooking big roasts, such as chicken or turkey, at the weekend, which will stretch to several meals. All you need to do is add some rice, potatoes and vegetables, and you are set. Use leftovers in a nutritious soup. A good cheat is to buy a good-quality ready-made chicken soup, and add the leftovers to it.
- Get some help, put your partner or children to work! With all hands on deck, a nutritious meal can be prepared in no time.

Chapter Nine

And There's More ...

No book with the word 'lifestyle' in the title would be complete without a few pointers on other aspects of healthy living. While a good diet under-pins every aspect of good health, there are other factors that need to be considered. In fact, no healthy eating programme will ever be successful unless you take steps to get the rest of your life on course. The effects of staying up all night, over-drinking, smoking too much, undergoing intense stress and sitting on the sofa all evening can be limited to some degree through a nutritious diet, but you'll never experience optimum health and wellbeing unless you are prepared to make some changes.

Sleep

Our lifestyles are dramatically different to those of our forebears. We get inadequate exercise, our lives are stressful and our 24-hour society means that we often undertake what were traditionally considered day-time tasks long into the night. When you can buy your groceries at 3 o'clock in the morning, get a haircut at midnight, shop on the Internet or do laun-dry at any time of the day or night, there is a temptation to fill every working hour with activity. The result? We have forgotten the importance of wind-ing down, and then we are puzzled about why we feel tired. In the past work had to end with the sunset, or shortly thereafter. Sleep was rightfully considered an essential part of daily life, and in the absence of much else to do in the late night, it took priority. While most of us would argue that it is still a priority, there are very few of us who manage to unwind successfully and get the required hours of sleep to meet our individual needs.

Many of us work and have little time to fit in housework and other house-hold responsibilities. Add to that the fact that working hours have increased dramatically, and we have a fairly disastrous situation. Relaxa-tion involves quick-fixes such as alcohol or fast-food meals, and then the customary plop in front of the television. At an appointed time - usually later than anticipated - we take ourselves off to bed, where we often find it difficult to sleep.

What to Do
Make sleep a priority. Only you will know how much you really need, but

between 7 and 10 hours is the norm for healthy adults. Children need much, much more.

- Stop working at least an hour before bedtime, and try reading something light.
- Make an early start: If you want to sleep at night, you need to get up early in the morning, every morning - including weekends. Regularity is important in keeping body rhythms constant.
- Early to bed: Make your lights-out time earlier rather than later. People who go to bed after midnight and get up late seem to get very little deep sleep.
- Get active: If you don't get enough exercise your body will be physically underused, causing disturbed or restless sleep. Sleep is a natural response to physical tiredness, and by increasing your intake of regular exercise you are likely to increase your amount of deep sleep.
- Take a warm (not hot) bath each night before bed, which will serve the dual purpose of relaxing you and also subconsciously 'washing away' the problems of the day.
- If you cannot get to sleep, switch on the light and read, or do something different, before you try to get back to sleep.
- If you are often too overtired to get to sleep, try taking short afternoon naps, to break the cycle.

Smoking

The evidence is indisputable: smoking lowers fertility, causes nutritional deficiencies, cancer and heart disease, and may shorten your life by over a decade.

Current anti-smoking measures might make you think that smoking is on the decrease, but that's not the case. Although smoking has fallen among the middle-aged and elderly in the UK since the 1960s, it has increased significantly among the young in recent years: 450 children start smoking every day.

What to Do
- As soon as you stop, your body begins to repair the damage done and you start to reduce the risk of smoking-related diseases. Eight to 10 years after quitting smoking, your risk of getting lung cancer or heart disease becomes the same as for someone who has never smoked.
- Stock up on antioxidants (see page 75), which can, in many cases, reverse the damage caused by smoking and prevent the formation of many types of cancers.
- For 70% of smokers, will-power is not enough. Nicotine replacement

therapy (in the form of patches, inhalers and gum) are twice as effective as will-power alone in kicking the habit.

Exercise

Despite the ever-increasing evidence that exercise is essential for health, most of us do little more than add exercise to an ever-growing to-do list. Six out of 10 women say they never take regular exercise, and men fared even worse in the exercise stakes.

What to Do
Walking It Off
Most of us don't have time for lengthy sessions in the gym; we need to find ways of incorporating exercise naturally into our lives. Many experts suggest walking more - getting off the train a stop early, or missing the bus altogether. You will get more accomplished: exercise makes you feel better and think more clearly, so you're more productive.

- Try walking in the morning. After a long, hard day we often lose the motivation to exercise.
- Take a lunchtime break: 20 minutes' brisk walking three or four times a week will greatly improve your cardiovascular fitness, help trim your body of excess fat and shape up your mind.
- Could walking be the new wonder exercise? Some experts think so. Australian researchers found that a brisk 25-minute walk at least three times a week helped to slow the rate of bone loss in postmenopausal women. An American study showed that a brisk 10-minute walk causes a shift in mood that quickly raises energy levels - and keeps them high for up to two hours.
- Walking just one mile (1.5 km) will burn up about 100 calories. So if you walk 30 minutes daily at a fairly brisk pace, you will easily burn up about 1,000 calories in a week. Two out of five of us are now obese, say the experts, so losing some weight can be no bad thing.

Stress

Most adults in today's society face considerable demands, and some of us cope better than others. Stress has become a buzzword, a peg on which to hang a multitude of symptoms and emotions that affect wellbeing, and certainly the term is now overused. It has become one of the most common causes of work-related litigation, and it's the single biggest reason for sick days and extended periods of time off work. In the UK, the Health and Safety Executive estimates stress is costing the economy £6.4 billion a year, and 70% of adults reported experiencing stress at work in the year 2000, up from 60% the previous year.

Most of us consider stress to be tension created by intolerable situations such as work, financial problems, relationship trouble, commuting and traffic jams, or bereavement, for example. Stress is certainly caused by all of these things, but there are many other issues that need to be considered.

First of all, stress is a response rather than a cause. Some people respond to external demands well, and experience few or no adverse effects. Other people have a lower 'stress threshold', which means that even the smallest trigger can set off a response, leaving them with a host of unpleasant symptoms. So there is a individual aspect to stress, which means that it is unique to every one of us. In terms of children, it's important to gauge what elements of their lifestyle may be stressful or creating a 'stress response', before deciding how to approach the problem.

What to Do
Learn to Relax
Take a course, find some leisure activities that you enjoy, take up yoga or go swimming. Anything that you enjoy, and which gives you time off from your busy life, is a good choice.

Stand back and take a look at your life. If you are doing too much, prioritise. What is important to you? What can be dropped? You can't be everything to everyone, and you'll never perform at your best if you are under too much pressure. Focus on the things that you enjoy. More importantly, look at your work-life, too. If every day is a challenge, it might be time for a change.

Exercise
This is one of the best ways to relieve stress, and essential for overall health (see page 113).

Learn to Manage Your Time
Clarify your values and goals. Imagine what you would like a close relative, friend or work colleague to say about you. Write this down as a 'personal statement' which you can refer to often. Do not be led by someone else's goals. Classify the activities that fill your week in terms of their importance and urgency. Many leisure activities and time with family and friends will be classified as important rather than urgent, but aim to spend as much time as possible doing these. This is a two-step process: you will stop committing yourself to things that are not important, and, gradually, fewer and fewer things will be urgent because you will have done them before they reach that point.

Treat Yourself
Think about the things that you enjoy that give you pleasure, make you laugh and help you to relax. An ideal treat might include time to read a book, spending the evening with someone you enjoy being with, a meal out, a film with a friend, a weekend away, a bar of scented soap or a night in watching a video.

Laugh
Humour is a powerful relaxation technique. Laughter triggers the release of endorphins - chemicals in the brain that produce feelings of euphoria. It also suppresses the production of cortisol, a hormone released when you are under stress which indirectly raises blood pressure by causing the body to retain salt.

Get Enough Sleep
Uninterrupted sleep is important to wellbeing. If you get less sleep than you need, you may wake feeling tense and incapable of coping with life's basic hassles. Avoid using alcohol or sleeping pills to help you get to sleep: they can interfere with your natural sleeping patterns and cause you to have a less restful night.

Write Down Your Concerns
Over a dozen studies have shown that if you write your problems out you can help relieve stress, improve your immunity, make fewer visits to the doctor and have a more optimistic view of life. Spend 20 minutes a day writing about your deepest thoughts and feelings. If you like you can throw the paper away afterwards, as this is said to encourage a sense of relief and a release from stress.

The Happiness Factor

A long-term study into happiness and wellbeing showed that people in less 'developed' countries are dramatically happier than those of us who seem to have everything. What's going wrong, then? The main culprit seems to be our over-scheduled lives. If you want to live well and longer in the 21st century, now is the time to make some changes to your lifestyle.

What to Do
● Mental wellbeing is enhanced by relaxation, but research shows that most people don't reach a relaxed physiological state when they are doing things that society generally considers relaxing, such as reading a newspaper, playing sport or watching television. The only real way to

get into a relaxed physiological state is to let your mind go into neutral. Experts recommend that we all take several 'mental rest stops' during the day, in order to lessen anxiety and help let go of stress and tension.

- Make stress-busting a priority in your life by learning to meditate or taking up yoga, for example. A Harvard University study showed that relaxation techniques can relieve even the most severe symptoms of PMS, short-circuit lower back pain and severe tension headaches, and reverse heart disease.

- Raise your happiness factor. Oxford psychologist Professor Michael Argyle argues that we need meaning and purpose in life to feel good, and he claims that a fulfilling job or leisure activity, sport, friends, a loving relationship and bringing up children can do just that.

- Cherish your leisure time. If you can't fit it in, make an appointment with yourself and write it down. Dr Carol Lassen, an American clinical psychologist, suggests that we need to find a reason to make room in our lives for leisure. It might be as simple as telling yourself that you want to live longer, or have better relationships with your family or friends. Whatever it is, it has to be something that is more important than work. To help you on your way, a new study shows that socially active adults are 34% less likely to die young than their less sociable counterparts.

Making Changes

Stuck for inspiration? Think of where you want to be and what you want to achieve in the next five years. Do you want to raise a family? Start on the road to a healthy old age? Find a successful career? Look good? Be happy? Write down your goals, and aim to meet them. With the help of this book, you'll be well on your way to making changes that will affect, for the better, the rest of your life. Why not grab an apple and start today?

Ten Top Tips for Healthy Eating

Experts agree the key to healthy eating is the time-tested advice of balance, variety, and moderation. In short, this means eating a wide variety of foods, based around the food pyramid and other elements of healthy eating, while cutting down on those foods that will do you no good at all. Avoid too eating too much of any one food (or drinking too much of one drink ...), which can undermine the healthy eating adventure.

These 10 tips can help you follow this advice while still enjoying the foods you eat:

1. Eat a variety of nutrient-rich foods. You need more than 40 different nutrients for good health, and no single food supplies them all. Base your daily diet around wholemeal breads and other whole carbohydrates, together with fruits, vegetables, some dairy produce, and lean meats, poultry and fish.
2. Follow the food pyramid as a guide (see page 33), but try to be imaginative. The same old foods prepared day in and day out will lead you to lose interest in a healthy way of eating. If you are stuck for ideas, buy a couple of cookery books and experiment with different types of foods and methods of preparing them.
3. Enjoy your food. Take pleasure in what you eat. Actively seek out delicious treats and sit down to savour them. Healthy eating does not have to be boring; in fact, it's quite the opposite! Most processed and ready-prepared foods are bland or over seasoned to make up for poor-quality ingredients. In time you'll get used to - and love - the natural sweetness and flavour of fresh, whole foods.
4. Make what you eat a priority. Plan meals in advance, consider what you are eating on a daily and weekly basis. No day will ever be perfect, but you can balance a few bad days or weeks by choosing fresh, wholesome foods the rest of the time. And if you know in advance what you are likely to be eating, and have the ingredients to hand, you'll be less tempted by unhealthy treats. If the going gets tough, take supplements to help ensure that you are getting what you need.
5. Don't be put off by the time element. Most of us assume that cooking healthy meals is much more time-consuming than it really is. In fact, when my book *Natural Healthcare for Children* was serialised in a national newspaper they put my healthy eating suggestions to the test and found that they took no more time than junk or fast-food alternatives.
6. Eat lots of different foods, but not too much of any one thing. Variety is,

as they say, the spice of life, and it's one way to ensure that you are getting all of the various nutrients you need. You'll also be less likely to become bored by your new way of eating.

7. Eat regularly. Blood sugar swings can play havoc with your emotions, your physical health, and your best intentions! Skipping meals will do you no good in the long run, so try to adopt a 'little and often' philosophy of eating.

8. Make food fun. Sit down with family and friends over delicious, healthy meals. Share recipes, prepare and cook food with your family, try different foods and ways of cooking them. Not only will you be setting an example and spreading the word that healthy eating is something to be enjoyed, but you'll have fun in the process.

9. Forget about weight-loss dieting. These diets don't work. If you eat a healthy, balanced variety of foods, your weight will even out over time. What's more, it will stay there!

10. Make changes gradually. Don't expect to revamp your eating habits overnight. Changing too much, too fast can get in the way of success. Begin to balance excesses or deficiencies with modest changes that can add up to positive, lifelong eating habits. Gradually add in a programme of self-care: start to get more sleep, try to give up smoking, work on learning to relax, find time for exercise and, above all, make time for yourself.

Further Reading

Cookbooks
River Cafe Cookbook Green, by Rose Gray and Ruth Rogers (Ebury Press)
The Complete Book of Food Combining, by Kathryn Marsden
  (Piatkus Books)
The Farmers' Market Cookbook, by Nina Planck (Hodder & Stoughton)
The Detox Cook, by Louisa J Walters, Aliza Baron Cohen and Adrian
  Mercuri (Kyle Cathie)

General Healthcare and Nutrition
Commonsense Healthcare for Children, by Karen Sullivan (Piatkus)
Organic Living in 10 Simple Lessons, by Karen Sullivan (Piatkus)
The Adam and Eve Diet, by Sarah Stacey and Roderick Lane
  (HodderHeadline)
The Optimum Nutrition Bible, Patrick Holford (Piatkus)
An Illustrated Guide to Vitamins and Minerals, by Karen Sullivan
  (HarperCollins/Element)
Superfoods, by Michael van Straten and Barbara Griggs (Dorling
  Kindersley, 1992)
Raw Energy, by Leslie and Susannah Kenton (Arrow, 1991)
The Women's Health Handbook, by Dr Marilyn Glenville (Piatkus, 2001)

Magazines
The Inside Story, Berrydales Publishers, 5 Lawn Road, London NW3 2XS
  Tel: 020 7722 2866. Fax: 020 7722 7685.
  E-mail: info@inside-story.com. Website: www.inside-story.com
  A monthly subscription newsletter for allergy sufferers and anyone on a
  restricted diet.
What Doctors Don't Tell You, 2 Salisbury Road, London SW19 4EZ
  Tel: 020 8944 9555. Fax: 020 8944 9888.
  E-mail: info@wddty.co.uk. Website: www.wddty.co.uk
  For news on medical issues, and publishers of several good books.

Exercise
Websites
A good site with lots of ideas: www.shapeup.org
Sport England: www.english.sports.gov.uk
Brilliant site with a self-assessment
  quiz, excuse 'busters' and ideas for
  keeping fit is Active for Life: www.active.org.uk/cgi-site/

Sleep
National Sleep Foundation, 1522 K Street, NW, Suite 500, Washington, DC 20005, USA. Fax: 1 202 347 3472.
Website: www.sleepfoundation.org
An American organisation with a website worth visiting.
Sleep Matters, Medical Advisory Service, PO Box 3087, London W4 4ZP
Helpline: 0208 994 9874

Websites
Sleepnet has loads of ideas for getting
to sleep and for dealing with sleep
disorders in people of all ages: www.sleepnet.com/
American Academy of
  Sleep Medicine: www.asda.org/public.htm
British sleep society: www.british-sleep-society.org.uk/

Stress
Institute of Stress Management, 57 Hall Lane, London NW4 4TJ
Tel: 0207 203 7355
International Stress Management Association (ISMA)
PO Box 348, Waltham Cross, EN8 8ZL
Tel: 07000 780430.
Email: info@isma.org.uk. Website: www.isma.org.uk

Good websites for Online readers
www.bc.sympatico.ca/Contents/health/
  This Canadian site has links to more than 5500 health and 'wellness'
  sites on the web. Over half of these are rated and reviewed.
www.veris-online.org/
  A brilliant site, with loads of information on research into the role of
  nutrition in health, with special attention paid to antioxidants.

Infants & Children's Health Page   www.cdc.gov/diseases/infant.html
Kidshealth: www.kidshealth.org
Fresh Fruit and Vegetable
  Information Bureau: www.ffvib.co.uk
American Society for
  Nutritional Sciences: www.nutrition.org/misc/ifora.shtml
The Coeliac Society: www.coeliac.co.uk
The Coronary Prevention Group: www.healthnet.org.uk

National Heart Forum:	www.heartforum.org.uk
Food and Drink Federation:	www.fdf.org.uk
Scottish Food and Drink Federation:	www.sfdf.org.uk
Sugar Bureau Scientific Information Service:	www.sugar-bureau.co.uk
Food Chain and Crops for Industry:	www.foresight.gov.uk/foodchain
Food Standards Agency:	www.foodstandards.gov.uk
Institute of Food Science and Technology:	www.ifst.org.uk
Campden and Chorleywood Food Research Association:	www.campden.co.uk
Institute of Consumer Sciences:	www.institute-consumer-sciences.co.uk
Leatherhead Food Research Assocation:	www.lfra.co.uk
Health in Focus:	www.healthinfocus.co.uk
Body Island:	www.bodyisland.com
Food Communications Information Service:	www.ucc.ie/fcis
Internet Health Library:	www.internethealthlibrary.com
Coffee Science Information Centre:	www.cosic.org
Manchester Metropolitan University:	www.fct.hollings.mmu.ac.uk
BBC On-Line Food:	www.bbc.co.uk/food
Institute of Food Research:	www.ifr.bbsrc.ac.uk
Dietitians UK:	www.dietitians.co.uk

Useful Addresses and Help On-line

Alcoholics Anonymous (AA)
UK helpline: 0845 7697555

Allergy Research Foundation
PO Box 18, Aylesbury
Bucks HP22 4XJ
Tel/Fax: 01296 655818
A site for health professionals

Association of Breastfeeding
  Mothers, 26 Holmshaw
London SE26 5TH
Tel: 0208 778 4769.
Fax: 0117 966 1788

British Allergy Foundation
Deepdene House
30 Belgrave Road, Welling
Kent DA16 3PY.
Tel: 020 8303 8525.
Fax: 020 8303 8792
Website:
  www.allergyfoundation.com

British Nutrition Foundation
High Holborn House,
52-54 High Holborn
London WC1V 6RQ.
Tel: 0207404 6504.
Fax: 0207404 6747
Email: postbox@nutrition.org.uk
Website: www.nutrition.org.uk/

British Society for Nutritional
  Medicine
Stone House,
9 Weymouth Street
London W1N 3FF.
Tel: 0207 436 8532

The Council for Nutrition
  Education and Therapy (CNEAT)
1 The Close, Halton, Aylesbury,
Buckinghamshire HP22 5NJ

The Food Magazine
94 White Lion Street
London N1 9PF
Tel: 020 7837 2250
For news on food and food issues

General Council and Register of
  Naturopaths, 2 Goswell Road
Street, Somerset BA16 0JG.
Tel: 01458 840072
Website: www.naturopathy.org.uk

Hyperactive Children's
  Support Group, 71 Whyke Lane
Chichester PO19 2LD.
Tel: 01243 551313
Fax: 01243 552019

Institute of Complementary
  Medicine (ICM)
PO Box 194, London SE16 7QZ
Tel: 020 7237 5165
Website: www.icmedicine.co.uk

Institute of Optimum Nutrition
Blades Court, Deodar Road
London SW15 2NU
Tel: 0208 877 9993 or contact its
founder, Patrick Holford on
www.patrickholford.com.
They also run the Food for the
Future Project, to promote the
importance of optimum nutrition
to children, adolescents, adults,
parents and teachers.

Mission Possible
Website:
 www.dorway.com/possible.html
International campaigners against
Aspartame

National Asthma Campaign
Providence House, Providence
Place, London N1 0NT.
Asthma helpline: 0345 010203
Tel: 0207 226 2269

National Childbirth Trust
Alexandra House, Oldham Terrace
Acton, London W3 6NH.
Helpline: 0208 992 8637

National Eczema Society
163 Eversholt Street, London
NW1 1BU. Tel: 0207 978 6278

National Institute of Medical
 Herbalists, 56 Longbrooke Street
Exeter, Devon EX4 6AH.
Tel: 01392 426022. E-mail: nimh
@ukexeter.freeserve.co.uk
Website: www.nimh.org.uk

Organic Farmers and Growers Ltd
50 High Street, Soham, Ely
Cambridgeshire CB7 5HP.
Tel: 01353 720250.
Fax: 01353 721571

Organic Food Federation
The Tithe House, Peaseland
Green, Elsing, East Dereham
NR20 3DY. Tel: 01362 637314.
Fax: 01362 637398

The Organic Gardening
 Catalogue

Riverdene Business Park
Molesey Road, Hersham, Surrey
KT12 4RG. Tel: 01392 253666
Fax: 01932 252707.
E-mail: chaseorg@aol.com
Website: www.organiccatalog.com

Pesticides Trust
Eurolink Centre, 49 Effra Road
London SW2 1BZ
Tel: 0207 274 8895
Fax: 0207 274 9084
Website: www:gn.apc.org/pestici-
destrust

Society for the Promotion of
 Nutritional Therapy, PO Box 47
Heathfield, East Sussex TN21 8ZX
01435 867007. (Send an SAE plus
fl1 for a copy of the register)

UK Register of Organic Food
 Standards (UKROFS)
Nobel House, 17 Smith Square
London SW1P 3JR
Tel: 0207 238 5915

The Vegan Society, Donald Watson
House, 7 Battle Roa
St Leonards-on-Sea, East Sussex
TN37 7AA. Tel:0845 458 8244.
Fax: 01424 717 064
E-mail: info@vegansociety.com
Website: www.vegansociety.com

The Vegetarian Society
Parkdale, Dunham Road
Altrincham, Cheshire WA14 4QG
Tel : 0161 925 2000.
Fax: 0161 926 9182
E-mail: info@vegsoc.org
Website: www.vegsoc.org

Index